RVing and Camping The Baja Peninsula

A Detailed Guide Book to Exploring Baja in
Your RV, Van, Car or Motorcycle

By Christopher and Lindsay Harvey

Founders, Owners of "Called To Wander" and "RVing Baja"

This Guide Book is dedicated to our friends Joe and Lilly and Bobby and Mary, two couples that taught us that Baja is best shared. From one, we were given the gift of confidence in making the journey on our own, and to the other we passed on this confidence.

We hope this Guide Book encourages you to share your Baja experience with others in a way that makes the world just a little smaller, kinder and a more enjoyable place to live and explore!

Table of Contents

Chapter 2: Camping Logistics in Baja

Be sure to join our Facebook group to participate in sharing and learning the most up-to-date information about a particular topic or area of interest.

Please note that all representations, facts and descriptions in this Guide Book are original and completed to the best of our ability. Any inaccuracies, discrepancies or incomplete information is the result of changes in circumstances and situations and is not intentional by the authors. Please feel free to contact us about any updates and suggestions you recommend for future editions to help us ensure as much accuracy as possible.

An Introduction to RVing and Camping the Baja Peninsula

You're likely reading this because you have heard of the beauty, adventure and relaxation that awaits in Baja, Mexico. The Baja peninsula offers all of this and so much more.

From world-class vineyards in Valle de Guadalupe to pristine beaches along the Bay of Concepcion and a handful of mountain ranges in between, the landscapes and natural beauty of Baja are remarkable.

And there's no shortage of wildlife to enjoy in the waters surrounding the peninsula. From swimming with whale sharks and sea lions to releasing baby sea turtles and watching humpback whales breach as you watch sunset on the beach - this is just the start of your Baja adventure!

The moment we first crossed the Tecate border in 2019, we found ourselves immediately hooked on Baja. And now, we've returned several times and always spend as much time as possible enjoying our favorite parts of Baja.

From spending time with wonderful new friends to eating delicious carnitas at our favorite taco stand to paddleboarding with sea lions, dolphins and whale sharks - we look forward to returning to Baja the moment we cross back into the US.

We've been sharing our Baja adventures on our YouTube channel and writing about Baja for years. Now we've decided to put everything we know about Baja together in this book so you can plan the adventure of a lifetime that will get you hooked on Baja!

Thanks for taking the time to see this spectacular part of the world through our eyes and we look forward to helping you find your own favorites as you wander the Baja Peninsula.

Who is this Guide Book for?

If you've heard about Baja and have been wanting to take a trip there but have been concerned about whether it is safe, whether you can find the basics such as power, water and sewer hookups or you're just interested in learning more of the logistics of how to travel in Baja, this Guide Book is for you!

We want to be clear that we believe this Guide Book will be an excellent resource for anyone looking to travel to Baja, Mexico. However, we have targeted most of the content in this book to those people who will explore the peninsula via camping.

But we're not limiting our definition of "camping" to just RV camping in Baja. Instead, we want to provide information to help you enjoy your time camping in Baja whether you are in an RV, are car camping or even bicycling or hiking the peninsula.

This Guide Book will be particularly useful if you are planning your first trip to Baja. However, we also hope to include information that may inspire you to travel to a new place on a subsequent visit.

Why travel to Baja?

We've already alluded to the fact that Baja is full of spectacular scenery, wonderful people and unique experiences. But there's more reason to travel to Baja than just those things.

There's a mystique about Baja, a sense of romanticism in thinking about this lesser inhabited and explored part of North America.

Baja usually evokes a sense of adventure and exploration. Although you can purchase most items using your credit card, there is still a sense of being lost in time as you drive through the small villages and towns in Baja.

Though most of the main roads are paved and you may not have to lug an extra jerry can of fuel around as those intrepid explorers did in the 1960s and 1970s, you can still find yourself driving down dirt roads more frequented by cows and coyotes than people, hiking to areas where you may stumble across unmarked cave and rock paintings and poking your head around some of the most pristine coral reefs on the planet.

Of course, you may also be attracted to the ease of living that many seek out on various beaches throughout the Baja peninsula. Whether you're looking for community among ex-pats at some of the more popular beaches, or you want to go off-grid and trek down 20 miles of washboard road for your own piece of solitude, Baja can accommodate your wishes.

Most people come to Baja to slow down their pace of life and are typically attracted to both formal and informal beach communities. Whether you want to boondock at beaches with no cell phone service or prefer to have a seaside view with a full hookup, life is easy in Baja.

The cost of living in Baja is also significantly less than that of most places in the United States and Canada. While you can usually find some way to go all out on a spending spree, you may be surprised how far your money will go in Baja if you are on a fixed income or just want to live frugally. Baja is very affordable and a great option if you're looking to save money during your travels.

And, of course, you can't beat the seasonal weather that offers warm winter nights along the Sea of Cortez to cool summer mornings along the Pacific Ocean. This is even more true if you are like a growing number of people who prefer to avoid the cold and snow of the Great North and would instead favor walking around barefoot in bathing suits on Christmas morning.

Baja is also full of adventure. We love standup paddleboarding and have no fewer than a dozen places in Baja where we enjoy taking our SUPs out. You can go marlin fishing in waters teeming with the prize fish, scuba diving and snorkeling and even swimming with the largest fish in the sea. Don't miss the opportunity to go whale watching as humpbacks, grey whales and even blue whales migrate along the coast.

On land, check out the various natural hot springs built into the side of the sea or in remote parts of the mountains. Go horseback riding to remote cave paintings, take multi-day hikes across the peninsula or enjoy some single track on your mountain bike or offroad tracks on your ATV.

From a sporting standpoint, you may be attracted to the surf along the Pacific Ocean or paddleboarding, kayaking or sailing the calm waters of the Sea of Cortez. Or perhaps you want to learn, or perfect, kiteboarding along the East Cape where the winds are consistently strong enough in the winter months to attract crowds of kite surfers.

Hike or mountain bike remote desert trails or ascend to the top of several challenging mountain peaks throughout the peninsula. Other than traditional winter sports, there really are not many outdoor activities that you can't do in Baja.

Disclaimers and General Principles About this Guide Book.

We have written this Guide Book from our personal travel experiences in Baja over multiple years. While it is impossible to provide completely accurate and up to date information, we have done our best to ensure that there are no surprises or discrepancies for you between what you read here and what you experience in Baja.

However, please note that information such as pricing, road conditions and even campground status may change. We have plans to continue to travel and update this Guide Book and invite you to join our Facebook group to participate in sharing and learning the most up-to-date information about a particular topic or area of interest.

Also note that we try to keep the tone of the Guide Book different from other sources of information by referencing "we" quite often. We want you to feel the same personal connection that we have with Baja, its people and landscapes, and we share factual information sometimes presented through our first-person experience.

We hope that you appreciate this touch and value the tips and information we present from our experience.

Disclaimer: We cannot claim liability for any information in this Guide Book that is inaccurate due to circumstances beyond our control. We assure you that the information we present is accurate to the best of our knowledge, ability and personal experience in traveling the Baja peninsula and we assure you that we have done our best to prepare you for the adventure of a lifetime in Baja!

Don't be a "Woody" - Keep Baja Beautiful

There's a long backstory as to why we say "Don't be a Woody." But essentially, we want you to always keep in mind that Baja is a terrifically beautiful place to visit. But it is wild and still quite limited in its resources.

In fact, most of what the people in Baja consume is produced elsewhere and shipped to the peninsula along the Federal Highway 1 by the vast number of semi-trucks you will come across in your travels.

As such, we are writing this book to promote tourism to Baja in the hopes that you will travel there responsibly and take into account the impact - both positive and negative - that you will have on the people and places that will exist long after you leave.

So please consider "Leave No Trace" principles when it comes to traveling in Baja. This concept will cover many aspects of travel including trying to minimize your waste, finding appropriate places to dispose of all wastewater and trash and seeking ways to make the most of every resource available - whether water, power or other such items you will use during your stay.

Whether this is your first visit or fifteenth, it is our hope that we can all work together to keep Baja beautiful so we can all continue to enjoy the many things we love about such an incredible place.

Prices, Distances & Current Conditions

Prices are indicated in US Dollars ("USD") and distances in miles (with parentheticals for kilometers) to try to standardize the information in this Guide Book. As the exchange rates constantly vary between USD, CAD and Mexican Pesos, it is up to you to research current exchange rates and do the basic math required to understand actual costs.

Further, road conditions and the availability of some campgrounds and key businesses we reference may also vary seasonally. Fall of 2022 brought several large storms, including Hurricane Kay, which brought large amounts of rain that washed out many roads and closed many businesses.

During our first visit to Baja in fall of 2019, Federal Highway 5 was being rebuilt from several storms in previous years that washed large sections of the highway away. It was an inconvenience, and rough at times, to follow several detours through the rocky terrain. However, it was safe and passable.

This is to say, as conditions and businesses that we reference in this Guide Book change, we will do our best to update the book and will include updates in our RVing and Camping the Baja Peninsula Facebook group.

Expert Tips

Additionally, while we feel the entire Guide Book gives you expert insight into how to travel Baja like a pro, we also have cutout sections we title "Expert Tip." In these sections, we provide even more detail on how we personally navigate situations and circumstances to make the most of our time traveling and camping in Baja.

Feel free to use or not use any of these special tips as it relates to your travels and let us know of any other tips or suggestions that you suggest other travelers use and we'll try to include these in future editions.

Boondocking and Alternative Camping Options

Another unique section of our Guide Book, the "Boondocking and Alternative Camping Options" provides some selective opportunities for you to escape the traditional campground environments in Baja to get off grid a little.

We have safely camped at each place we mention. However, because boondocking conditions and permissions change, we do not provide specific details other than a general description of each place.

You should do due diligence, either by visiting in person or checking the latest camping app reviews, to ensure these camping spots are still available. We will update future editions, and include additional recommendations, based on any information we collect in subsequent travels or as suggested by other travelers.

Volunteering Opportunities

Finally, we believe that it is important to connect with and experience the local community as much as possible when traveling in Baja. Because we believe that it is important to invest in understanding and participating in local communities as you travel, we have highlighted some great volunteer opportunities where we feel you can have an impact during your stay.

Whether you have a heart for children, dogs, sea turtles or want to make the environment a little cleaner and more sustainable - there are tons of great opportunities to get involved with individuals and organizations in Baja. We'll share a few of our favorites throughout this book.

Additional Resources & Information

The adventure is endless in Baja. Each time you visit you will experience new opportunities that will likely lead you to love the peninsula as much as we do! Whether this is your first visit or one of many, we hope that you will appreciate the information we provide you to make the most of the opportunity to visit a truly unique and wonderful place.

If you have purchased and are reading the PDF version of this Guide Book, we have given you the added value of linking to tons of additional resources, including products and services, that will enhance your study and preparation.

You may also find additional and perhaps more updated information at these resources:

RVing and Camping the Baja Peninsula Facebook Group

RVing Baja Website

Affiliate Disclaimer: Note that some links may be affiliate links, meaning we receive a small commission at no cost to you if you choose to purchase the products and services we recommend. Of course, we're only recommending those things that we ourselves use and suggest you consider when traveling and camping in Baja!

CHAPTER 1

Planning Your Trip/ Considerations/How Life In Baja Works

The following sections of the Guide Book will assist you in some of the planning logistics and understanding the way of life of traveling and camping in Baja.

We're covering the key topics that apply to you regardless of what type of vehicle or how you plan to visit Baja.

The Geography of Baja California

Baja California is a peninsula that runs nearly 1,000 miles (1,600 km) from its northern border with the United States to "Lands End," the very southern tip in Cabo San Lucas.

Its western side is hemmed in by the Pacific Ocean, while the Sea of Cortez (also known as Gulf of California) runs along its eastern edge.

At the very southern end of the peninsula, these two bodies of water meet along what is known as the "East Cape," one of the world's most ecologically diverse regions.

The peninsula is divided geographically and politically into two states. The northern state, Baja California ("BC"), includes all of the border cities such as Tijuana, Tecate and Mexicali as well as more popular destinations such as San Felipe and Ensenada.

The southern state, Baja California Sur ("BCS"), begins about halfway down the peninsula with a small industrial town of Guerrero Negro and includes only a few cities such as La Paz and Los Cabos (Cabo

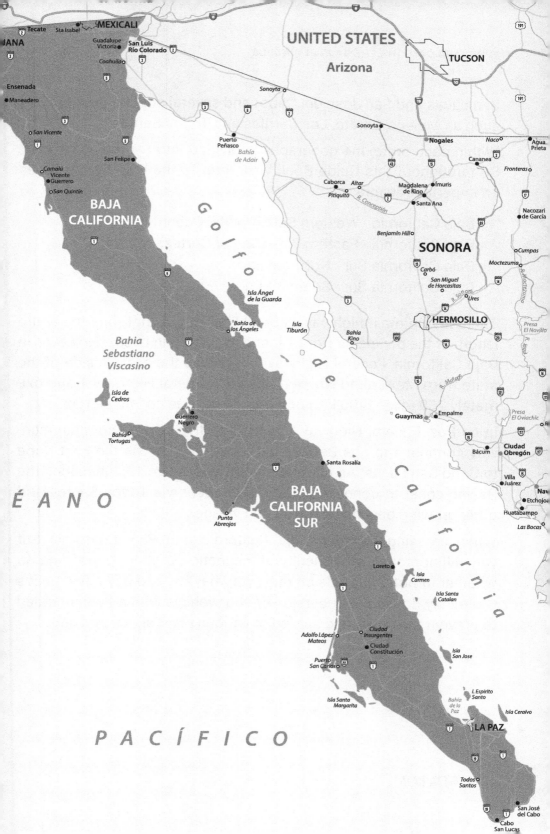

San Lucas and San Jose del Cabo) and several popular destinations such as Mulege, Loreto, Los Barriles and Todos Santos.

Within each state, the geography is divided into two basic regions. So throughout this Guide Book we'll refer to the Baja Peninsula as an imperfect quadrant.

- Baja California - Western Side (Pacific Ocean)
- Baja California - Eastern Side (Sea of Cortez)
- Baja California Sur - Northern End
- Baja California Sur - Southern End

There is one main highway, Federal Highway 1, that runs the entire length of the peninsula from Tijuana to Cabo San Lucas. However, in Baja California, Federal Highway 5 connects the eastern side of the state from Mexicali to where it ties into Federal Highway 1 approximately 250 miles (400 km) and then continues on into La Paz.

In La Paz, Federal Highway 1 splits into two parts. The main highway continues to Los Barriles before cutting across the East Cape to Cabo San Lucas. An alternate highway, Mexico 19, runs along the Pacific coast to connect to Cabo San Lucas via Todos Santos and other growing beachside towns and villages.

When crossing between Baja California and Baja California Sur you will approach an Agricultural Inspection Station. Depending on whether or not a guard is on duty, you may have to pay a few pesos while they douse the underside of your vehicle with a fluid intended to prevent the unwanted spread of various plant seeds and soil.

When To Visit Baja

Like most decisions in life, this one is up to personal preference. However, by far the most popular time to visit Baja is from the fall to the spring when the air temperatures tend to be more favorable and the threat of severe storms and hurricanes has passed.

The influx of campers generally begins in November and typically most people will clear out of the peninsula before Semana Santa, or the Holy Week, which occurs the week before Easter.

Winter air temperatures during this time are incredibly pleasant, water temperatures are warm enough to enjoy and marine life is most active during these months.

However, Semana Santa belongs to the locals. During this week most businesses shut down or reduce their hours as friends and families head out to spend the week on their favorite beaches. You are always welcome to be a part of the festivities. But this week is loud and your private spot on the beach won't be very private!

Temperatures also begin to rise rapidly beginning in April and continue through summer and into early fall. Hurricane season kicks off in mid-May and continues through November 30. And while torrential rain is rare, Baja is a desert peninsula that does not handle massive rainfall very well.

If you plan to visit Baja during the summer be mindful of the weather and an increase in the number of bugs around. Most travelers spend the summer months on the western side of the peninsula where the cooler Pacific Ocean provides some respite from otherwise hot weather.

But if you want to experience warmer water and fewer people camping in Baja, summer will be a great time to visit.

What to See and Do in Baja

We believe that Baja is paradise and aside from an inviting climate and incredibly friendly people, the peninsula offers all sorts of great activities. It is a mecca for outdoor enthusiasts who seek to do everything from surfing and kiteboarding to hiking and horseback riding.

These are a few of the top reasons many people consider visiting Baja.

Surfing

Surfing is popular throughout Baja along the western, Pacific Ocean side of the peninsula. Some of the more popular places to surf are along the beaches between Tijuana and Ensenada, which are within a short drive from the US border, and along the beaches around San Juanico and Todos Santos in the southern part of the peninsula.

However, there are lots of other places where you can find great surf — often in mostly secluded beach spots that may or may not be accessible without 4x4.

Standup Paddleboarding & Kayaking

While the Pacific coast of Baja offers a surfer's paradise, the eastern coast along the Sea of Cortez tends to attract those people who enjoy flatwater activities such as standup paddleboarding, snorkeling and kayaking.

The water in the Sea of Cortez tends to be calm and there are lots of sheltered bays and coves where you can spend endless days exploring the landscape and the underwater world. One of our personal favorite activities is to pack our snorkeling gear on our SUPs and head out to find our own tropical reefs to observe.

Some towns along the Sea of Cortez, such as Loreto and La Paz, have several companies that offer a variety of kayaking tours ranging from a few hours to multi-day adventures.

Snorkeling and Scuba Diving

Jacques Cousteau once said that the Sea of Cortez was the "aquarium of the world" because of all of the diversity of marine life found in its waters.

Although snorkeling and scuba diving may not be the first thing that comes to mind when you picture the ruggedness of Baja, if you enjoy exploring the underwater world then Baja has a lot to offer. Informally, you can snorkel virtually anywhere you camp along the Sea of Cortez.

Some of our favorite places are along the Bay of Concepcion and further south in Cabo Pulmo along the East Cape. In both places, and many in between, you can often walk a few feet from your campsite to the water's edge and find yourself on a reef within minutes.

Cabo Pulmo has some of the most pristine reefs in the world and attracts snorkeling and diving enthusiasts from everywhere. And if you are looking for a more formal experience, particularly in La Paz and Cabo Pulmo you can hire guides to take you on half, full or multi-day snorkeling and diving trips.

One of our favorite tours takes you to snorkel with whale sharks in the morning and then sea lions and a variety of reef fish along the La Isla Espirito Santo.

Mountain Biking & Hiking

Several mountain ranges run through the Baja peninsula creating a great opportunity to get off the beaten path to enjoy some unique mountain biking and hiking.

Whether your goal is to hike to the top of Pichacho del Diablo, the highest peak in Baja, or to simply wander through a nearby arroyo (dry riverbed) to see how far it goes, hiking is a great way to see parts of Baja that many people miss.

In fact, some of our favorite trails begin at our favorite beachside camping spots and take you on a meandering path along the coast that offers spectacular views most people do not see!

There is also great mountain biking that you can do, particularly in Baja California Sur. The areas around Todos Santos and La Ventana have attracted avid mountain bikers who have helped to create extensive trail systems that continue to attract more and more riders.

Fishing

By definition, the Baja peninsula is surrounded on 3 sides by saltwater. This makes it an ideal destination if you enjoy fishing. Sportfishing is very popular on both the Sea of Cortez and Pacific Ocean sides of the peninsula.

Depending on the time of year and location, you could expect to catch everything from mahi mahi and roosterfish to a variety of tuna, mackerel, snapper, grouper and, of course, the prized marlin.

Cabo San Lucas is the marlin hot spot and mecca for most sportfishing. However, there are pockets of fishing activity in places like Los Barriles, Loreto and Mulege along the Sea of Cortez and several bays and estuaries along the Pacific Ocean.

Some of the most successful fishing charters we've come across have been out of San Carlos along Magdalena Bay.

Marine Wildlife in Baja

Wildlife in Baja is one of the main attractions for many visitors to the peninsula. Although the land is mostly desert, marine life abounds in every direction and season.

You can swim with whale sharks and sea lions in La Paz during the winter months. And grey, humpback and fin whales migrate along the coast during early spring in such abundance that you can watch them spout and breach from the shore.

A variety of sea turtles also come ashore in several places where turtle sanctuaries and hatcheries provide both an educational and unique hands-on experience for visitors to release baby sea turtles into the sea.

The Mexican government is quite protective of marine species and you will be limited in what you can and should experience on your own. However, there are plenty of reasonably priced tour operators in every destination where you can interact with the marine wildlife of Baja.

History

Baja California has been inhabited for the past 9,000-10,000 years. As such, there is a tremendous amount of history documented through everything from primitive cave paintings to colonial towns lined with cobblestone streets and that house beautiful Spanish missions.

You can explore many pieces of history on your own, particularly if you have an ATV or 4x4 vehicle. And there are several places, such as the idyllic oasis town of San Ignacio, where you can sign up for multi-day mule rides to get into the heart of ancient history in Baja.

Whether you want to stroll the streets of Todos Santos or Loreto, two quintessential colonial towns identified as "Pueblos Magicos" by the Mexican government, or find yourself exploring more remote and less-visited areas such as the Comondus, if history is your thing you'll not be disappointed with Baja.

In fact, some of our favorite historical locations are so intertwined with the present that you may not realize that you are walking where John Wayne and members of the Rat Pack used to spend their time or that you may find yourself paddling along the shoreline to discover thousand-year old handpainted rocks visible only from the water at low tide.

Culture

Along with a rich history comes a layering of culture that is unique to the Baja peninsula. It has been related to us over the years that Baja is often overlooked by mainland Mexico in part because of its geographical separation from the rest of the country but also because things are so much different in Baja than on the mainland.

Baja has developed its own identity and even between the two states of Baja California, you will find cultural differences that make each place unique. From different foods found only in certain areas to a faster or slower pace of life, Baja has plenty of culture to immerse yourself in while there.

Art lovers fall in love with Todos Santos, which teems with creatives, and spills over into places like El Triunfo and San Antonio in the nearby Sierra de la Laguna mountain ranges in the south.

And food aficionados can enjoy everything from a remarkable breakfast at Dona Esthela's Kitchen in Valle de Guadalupe, which has drawn the critical acclaim of the likes of Anthony Bordain, to the most delicious carnitas at Asadero Dany's in Mulege or papas rellenos in Los Barriles or La Paz.

If you're looking for nightlife, music and entertainment you'll find everything you're looking for (and quite a bit you may not!) in Ensenada and San Felipe in the north and in La Paz and Cabo San Lucas in the south.

Key Baja Terminology and Conversions

Although being fluent in Spanish would be helpful when traveling anywhere in Mexico, there are some key terms you should know that will make your travels more comfortable and convenient.

While you will be able to get by with English in most circumstances, knowing how to communicate with locals or at least what to expect in some situations will add value to your experience.

The following terms are many, though not fully inclusive, of the key words and phrases that will help you during your travels.

Key Words and Phrases

- **Tope** - A speed bump, "hump" or other form of slowing drivers down
- **Arroyo** - A dry riverbed, often used for camping
- **Vado** - A dip in the road, often filled with water during the rainy season
- **Agua Purificados** - Purified water dispensaries
- **Manguera** - A hose for filling your water tank
- **Malecon** - The boardwalk or walkway along the seaside
- **Garrafon** - A container for water, usually 5 gallons (~20 liters)
- **Palapa** - A simple thatch hut made from palm leaves to provide shade and protection from the wind when camping
- **FMM (Forma Migratoria Multiple)** - The "visa" that allows you to travel throughout Mexico
- **Curvas Peligrosas - "Dangerous curves"** in the road, particularly downhill
- **Cero** - Translated to "zero" and used by fuel attendants when starting to pump your gas
- **Alto** - Stop. Usually placed on an octagonal shaped red sign
- **Despacio** - Slow. As in slow down when you are driving through

Baja Itinerary Options

It is hard to put a set timeframe on how long you should visit Baja California, where you should go and what you should do during that timeframe. In fact, every time we have visited Baja we've stayed for a minimum of 4-5 months.

But we have also traveled with friends who had a long weekend to spend with us between the surfing beaches north of Ensenada and the vineyards of Valle de Guadalupe (which makes for a great short first trip to Baja!).

And we've met others who have spent a week or two of their Thanksgiving, Christmas or Spring break racing down to the Bay of Concepcion and La Paz in Baja California Sur to maximize their time in the sunshine, sand and salt water.

We also have friends who make an annual trek south to spend a few days in early spring interacting with the grey whales before they make their way toward Alaska.

We would say that Baja, like most other places in the world, is best experienced at a slower pace and an open timeline. You may be surprised to find that a place you expected to spend a week may be accomplished in just a few nights. While you'll learn of other places you didn't realize existed until you arrived and spent two weeks.

RV living in Baja, in general, is easy. So whether you only have a long weekend, a few weeks or even a few months you will make the most of your time no doubt.

Here are a few highlights that we would suggest with a variety of 2-week itineraries:

Option 1 - Two Weeks in Baja California

If you only had 2 weeks to spend in Baja and you wanted to make the most of this time, you could easily spend your time exploring the best of the northern state.

Crossing either at Tijuana or Tecate, you could start your time in Baja with a few days each in Valle de Guadalupe and along the beaches in and around Ensenada. You could then drive south along Federal Highway 1 and stop off at your favorite sleepy beachside towns such as San Quintin, or enjoy the surreal desert landscapes of places like Catavina.

Federal Highway 1 will meet with Federal Highway 5 at the southern end of Baja California and you should absolutely continue a little further to take the drive out to the Bay of Los Angeles.

The Bay of Los Angeles will warrant a few days in itself, just for the scenic drive out and back. Relax, fish or catch a wildlife tour or two before heading back north.

This time take Highway 5 north along the Sea of Cortez. In what is perhaps the best stretch of pavement in all of Baja, Highway 5 will give you ample opportunity to pull over for a day or two here or there in places like Gonzaga Bay and Puertecitos.

And by the time you reach San Felipe, you may be ready to enjoy the benefits of a more populated city with a bustling Malecon, tons of great restaurants and bars and plenty of activities to round out your adventure.

Of course, you could do this same loop in reverse if you'd like.

Option 2 - Two Weeks in Baja California Sur

If you have your sights set on spending most of your time in Baja California Sur (BCS), you are not alone. This is by far our favorite of the two states and there is quite a bit of a different feel to it.

Of course, you need to plan for at least 2 drive days in each direction to safely transit between the border and your final destinations in BCS.

One of the most popular itineraries for Baja California Sur is simply to race south until you reach the Bay of Concepcion and then hole up on your favorite beach until it's time to head north again.

You'll miss out on much of what the rest of the state has to offer. But you won't regret the time you spend on the Bay of Concepcion.

A more thorough route would involve timing your trip so you could stop for a day or two near Guerrero Negro so that you could spend some time with the grey whales in the Laguna Ojo de Liebre.

From there, spend a night or two in San Ignacio where you can camp in the square or along the river and take in some kayaking or paddle-boarding through the desert oasis. Continue to Mulege for a night or two, timing a Saturday morning trip to Asadero Dany's for his weekly carnitas offering.

Enjoy the quaint little town and continue on to the Bay of Concepcion for a few days. But don't get stuck there! The next stop is Loreto, one of the Pueblos Magicos, well preserved and popular among tourists of all kinds.

A few days later, keep heading south on the longest stretch until you get to La Paz. La Paz and the surrounding beaches could keep you entertained for days on their own - between swimming with whale sharks and sea lions, walking and eating your way along the Malecon and enjoying the laid-back city life of the southern state's capital.

Take a loop around the East Cape - starting with a drive through the mountains to Los Barriles and then spending a few days in Cabo Pulmo if you have a rugged enough RV to handle miles of unpaved and unmaintained roads.

Pop out of that natural beauty for a quick peek at Los Cabos (though don't expect to find proper camping in either San Jose del Cabo or Cabo San Lucas) before starting your northward trek.

Before you start backtracking you can spend another few days around Todos Santos, either in the town itself or at its neighboring beachside communities of El Pescadero and/or Playa Los Cerritos.

Of course, this far south will take a few days to trek back to the border. And you can break up the drive at any of your favorite places from your way south.

Or consider making a detour to San Carlos, Adolfo Lopez Mateos or Laguna San Ignacio to head out on a whale-watching tour if you didn't do so on your way south.

Option 3 - Baja California in its entirety

Combining shorter trips in both Baja California and Baja California Sur, you can see how difficult it would be to enjoy and experience the entire peninsula in a matter of weeks. So we'll let you determine if it's even possible for you to combine our suggested itineraries for both the northern and southern states.

Although we usually spend a few months stationary between a few of our favorite beaches, even if you were to try and see it all in a month you will understand why we take so much time to enjoy RVing in Baja.

After our first trip, which was more or less a 4-month whirlwind tour of trying to see and do everything we could, we decided our next time to Baja we wanted to spend more time in Mulege and camping along the beaches of the Bay of Concepcion and in and around La Paz. So we customized our next itinerary to do just that.

However long you have, you will find that it is never long enough and we encourage you to consider returning to Baja as often and for as long as you can!

What To Expect at Campgrounds in Baja

One of the most common concerns that first-time Baja campers have is the availability and condition of campgrounds throughout the peninsula. And while Baja maintains its rugged and rustic persona, there are plenty of great campground options scattered about between the two states that make RVing in Baja relatively convenient.

In fact, there are a handful of Baja campgrounds that are in much better shape than their counterparts north of the border!

Cost of Campgrounds in Baja

Campgrounds in Baja will range in cost from $5-$10 USD on the low side to upwards of $25-$35 USD or more on the high side. Of course, the price of the campground varies on where it is and what amenities are offered.

Campgrounds in the popular towns of San Felipe, Los Barriles, Todos Santos and La Paz will be on the higher side due to the demand placed on them by travelers eager to winter in warmer weather where they have a lot of the infrastructure and the niceties of home.

And even small towns such as Mulege, San Ignacio and Loreto in Baja California Sur have seen the pricing of their campgrounds rise in recent years due to an influx of travelers and making up for the slowdown from the pandemic.

But you can still find basic seaside campgrounds in places like Alisitos and San Quintin for around $10 USD per night that offer little more than dry camping.

If you are planning to camp in formal campgrounds throughout your camping in Baja adventure, we would advise that you budget around $25-$30 USD per night to avoid going over budget. If you plan to stay in one place for a long period of time you can always negotiate long-term camping rates that are much more favorable.

RVING BAJA

But if you are considering this, particularly between January and March, be sure to make reservations well in advance.

During our trips to Baja, we average around $10 USD per night for camping. But that includes the few nights per month we spend in a formal campground with both the free camping we do and the few places where you may spend $10-$15 USD to camp on the beach (particularly along the Bay of Concepcion).

But we always budget around $20 USD per night to account for the fact that some destinations - particularly Valle de Guadalupe, San Felipe, La Paz, Los Barriles and the Todos Santos area - are easily going to be at or above that amount.

Baja Campground Amenities

We'll go into much more detail about specific campgrounds we recommend throughout Baja in later chapters. But when it comes to amenities, you can expect everything from basic dry camping and limited additional offerings to having full hookups, clean hot showers and laundry facilities, fast WiFi and even some campgrounds offering pools and hot tubs.

As with campgrounds in the US and Canada, just because a campground advertises WiFi or hot showers does not necessarily mean it meets your standards.

We've included the following icons in each campground listing.

 20/30 Amp Electric   Water Hookup

 Sewer Hookup   Big Rig Friendly

 Pet Friendly   Wifi Availability

 Laundry   Shower

 Pool/Spa   Gated/Security

Power, Water and Sewer Hookups

Campgrounds in Baja will vary in what they offer by way of power, water and sewer hookups. Chances are you'll end up getting most of what you need out of each campground where you stay.

But we'll cover a little more of the details of what to expect below.

Electric Hookups

Electric hookups in Baja vary in quality. Typically you will be offered a 20 amp hookup with some campgrounds offering 30 amp. We have never seen a full 50 amp electric hookup. So be aware of your particular needs and what you can and cannot run if you are used to a 50 amp hookup.

We also would advise that you consider investing in a decent surge protector and a multimeter so that you can test the electricity at each campsite prior to connecting your shore power.

We've seen campsites ranging from the low 100V to over 130V, both extremes of which would harm your RV electrical appliances. And in some campgrounds, the electric post has been melted or is being held together by tape or exposed wires.

However, generally speaking, you will find that power in Baja will meet your needs. Most people camp in Baja during fall, winter and spring when the temperatures are cooler and you are not as inclined to need to run your AC often or at all.

But we've also had a few hot nights in a campground where everyone ran their AC and the campground experienced a blackout.

Water Hookups

Water hookups will be reliable at most campgrounds throughout Baja. However, we do not encourage you to drink the water from the water source. We always rely on purified water for our drinking water.

But we shower and do dishes with water from our city water

hookups. And before we leave a campground we always fill our fresh water tank with water to which we add a few drops of bleach just to be safe.

Sewer Hookups

When it comes to sewer hookups, some campgrounds are better than others. We learned that some campgrounds use a very rudimentary septic tank system using the ground to filter wastewater.

While others have systems in place to recycle and reuse wastewater throughout the campground landscaping.

Most campgrounds fall somewhere in between. If they offer sewer hookups or have a dump station, you can expect it to work as you need it to. But don't expect much more.

Car and Tent Camping In Baja

Although this Guide Book is targeted toward travelers with some kind of self-contained camper or trailer, we do want to point out that Baja is incredibly friendly toward car and tent camping.

You'll find many places, including formal and informal campgrounds, where there are dedicated spaces for tent campers. Often, tent camping is offered at a reduced rate and in dedicated spaces in formal campgrounds.

But more often than not you may find yourself on a beach, in the desert or somewhere you will recognize how inviting and tent-friendly the camping options are.

Do be mindful that you should not count on tent camping in urban areas outside of the campgrounds that may or may not offer it. We do not in any way promote or encourage "stealth camping" and will do our best to indicate in future editions which campgrounds offer car and tent camping options in urban areas.

Crossing the Border

Arguably the most intimidating part of planning your Baja camping adventure is figuring out how the border crossing works.

Between the paperwork, waiting in lines and the inspections that invariably happen, it can be a bit overwhelming and we've known people who actually turned around and canceled their Baja plans last minute because of this!

However, we have crossed multiple times and have some tips and advice to help you plan your journey - starting at the border.

We'll cover each of these items in more detail below. But know that you will need to have the following paperwork when crossing into Mexico:

Required Documents

- Forma Migratoria Multiple (FMM)
- Passport or Passport card
- Vehicle Insurance
- Vehicle Registration
- Boat/Additional Vehicle Registration (if applicable)
- Pet vaccination records (if applicable)

What Border Crossings Are There (And Which One Is Best?)

There are 6 opportunities to cross the border into Baja. From west to east, these are the border crossings between the US and Baja, Mexico.

Border Crossings

- San Ysidro (San Diego/Tijuana)
- Otay Mesa (San Diego/Tijuana)
- Tecate
- Calexico West (Mexicali)
- Calexico East (Mexicali)
- Andrade (Los Algodones)

By far, our favorite border crossings are Tecate and Calexico East Depending on which direction you are traveling from and where you intend to go in Baja, you may consider either a convenience.

Tecate is small and quiet. So depending on the time of day, this could work in your favor. Potrero County Park, on the US side, has a campground around 15 minutes from the border where many travelers will spend the night prior to making an early morning crossing.

Although there are parking lots on the US side where you can park and walk your paperwork through both sides of the border, typically you can pull right up to the Mexican border and agents will assist you in completing all paperwork and inspections.

Our other favorite border crossing is Calexico/Mexicali East. When we travel to Baja we typically come from Arizona and this is the first convenient crossing from the east. Although it can be congested at times, we have had nothing but positive experiences crossing here.

Here you will be asked to park your vehicle and go inside to complete your paperwork. But we've not seen a line and the entire process and inspection is completed in a matter of a few minutes.

If you are coming from San Diego and either do not want to drive east or are planning to follow the Pacific coastline as you head south, then either San Ysidro or Otay Mesa will put you in the heart of Tijuana. This can be a bit overwhelming at first as you need to work your way toward Mexican Federal Highway 1, which will then lead you south.

If you are traveling from the east or have plans to visit San Felipe, then crossing at either Calexico/Mexicali crossing will be most convenient.

A more indirect route, the Andrade crossing into Los Algodones will connect you to the easternmost edge of Baja which will then lead you toward Mexican Federal Highway 5 to continue your journey south. Most people who cross here do so for dental and medical tourism in Los Algodones as it is not a convenient crossing to explore the rest of Baja.

Regardless of where you cross, we recommend that you download the BorderTraffic app on your mobile device to be able to check the wait times and plan the most efficient crossing.

Border Crossing	Hours	Address	Banjercito	Accepts Sentri
San Ysidro (San Diego/ Tijuana)	24/7	725 E San Ysidro Blvd, San Diego, CA 92173	Y	Y
Otay Mesa (San Diego/ Tijuana)	24/7	Garita Internacional, 22430 Tijuana, Baja California, Mexico	Y	Y
Tecate	6AM - 10PM	Pdte. Lázaro Cárdenas 190, Primera, 21400 Tecate, B.C., Mexico	Y	Y
Calexico West (Mexicali I)	24/7	Calz. de los Presidentes S/N, Río Nuevo, 21120 Mexicali, B.C., Mexico	Y	Y
Calexico East (Mexicali II)	6AM - 12AM	Avenida Abelardo L Rodriguez S/N, Alamitos, 21210 Mexicali, B.C., Mexico	Y	Y
Andrade (Los Algodones)	6AM - 10PM	Calle Mariano Lee 150, Vicente Guerrero, 21970 Vicente Guerrero, B.C., Mexico	Y	Y

Forma Migratoria Múltiple (FMM)

The Forma Migratoria Múltiple, more commonly referred to as the FMM, is your formal ticket into Mexico. Although it has been referred to as a "visa," it is not in fact a formal visa.

You will need a valid Passport or passport card to complete the FMM application and to present it at the Mexican Immigration Office (INM) upon crossing.

Regardless of which border crossing you take, you will be required to pay for an FMM that will be valid for your entire stay for up to 180 days. If you plan to stay for 7 days or less you will not be charged for the FMM but you will still need to have one and present it at the INM.

You can complete your application for your FMM online or in person. We have done both and while completing the FMM online seems like it would be more convenient, you still have to stop and enter the Mexican Immigration office either way.

Additionally, if you do complete the process online be sure to print BOTH the FMM AND the receipt. If you fail to present both to INM they will require you to complete the process and pay a second time.

This reason alone makes it worthwhile just to complete the FMM in person at whichever border crossing you choose.

Recently, FMMs cost around 600 pesos (around $30 USD) per person. You will want to keep it on hand at all times as you will be asked to present your passport and FMM at frequent military checkpoints throughout Baja.

You are free to cross back and forth multiple times with one FMM as long as the FMM is valid. And you will likely not be asked to return it upon crossing back into the US.

Passport or Passport Card

It should not be a surprise that you will be required to present your passport at the border. Be sure to keep this handy along with your FMM as you will be asked to present it at virtually every military checkpoint throughout the peninsula.

We fold our FMM into our passport and tuck them away in a basic passport holder that we hide away in a special place. We only retrieve the passports during travels when we know we are approaching a military checkpoint.

Vehicle/Auto Insurance

Although auto/RV insurance is mandatory when driving in Mexico, you will likely not be asked to present proof of insurance when crossing the border. However, you will want to ensure that you have adequate insurance in the event of an accident as the Mexican government takes automobile accidents incredibly seriously.

Expert Tip

We make copies of our passports and laminate them prior to entering Mexico. Although we have never had any issues with police, military or immigration officers retaining our passports, we like to have a "backup" in the event our original passports are lost or stolen. Of course, if lost or stolen, you should file a police report and/or report this immediately to the nearest Consulate office, which would be located in either Tijuana or San Jose del Cabo.

Although the Mexican government only requires you to carry liability insurance to cover any damage or injury to other drivers, it is not much more expensive to have full comprehensive coverage.

Insurance is not terribly expensive and becomes even more affordable the longer your policy is in effect. We typically purchase a 6-month policy even if we only plan to stay 4-5 months because it is cheaper to purchase the 6-month policy.

There are several insurance brokers that will allow you to purchase Mexican auto/RV insurance prior to your arrival at the border. These are the largest and most well-known:

Mexican Auto Insurance Brokers

- Baja Bound
- MexPro
- Baja Auto Insurance
- Discover Baja Travel Club

You can purchase insurance when crossing the border. However, this can be a complicated process and is typically more expensive. We recommend purchasing insurance prior to crossing the border which gives you the ability to print your documents as well.

Expert Tip

Before purchasing Mexican auto insurance, check with your US or Canadian insurance company to determine the inclusions and limits of your specific policy.

For example, our US policy will cover any theft or damage to our RV while in Baja so we always purchase Mexican "liability only" policies for our time in Baja.

Also, be sure that you have insurance on each vehicle you bring with you - whether tow vehicle, ATV, boat, motorcycle, etc. You can often bundle insurance with your primary vehicle/RV/van and your additional vehicles when you purchase Mexican auto insurance.

We have used Baja Bound each time we have traveled to Baja and have had nothing but wonderful things to say about the company, rates and customer service.

Although we have fortunately not been involved in any accidents, we have called their customer service on several occasions to gain a better understanding of our policy under certain circumstances.

They find the most competitive rates for the leading Mexican auto insurance companies and will talk you through each part of your policy to make the best decision about how much coverage you may or may not need.

Vehicle Registration
Upon arriving at the INM office, or when pulling up to the border itself, you will be asked to present your documentation. One of the items that will likely be checked is your vehicle registration.

Be sure to have a copy of your current vehicle registration and ensure that it does not expire before the date on your FMM. You must have a valid registration for every day you plan to spend in Mexico, whether only in Baja or in the mainland.

Boat/Additional Vehicle Registration
In addition to having adequate insurance for each additional motorized vehicle or boat, you will also want to make sure you have a valid title and registration for each. This includes towed vehicles, motorcycles/mopeds, dirt bikes and ATVs.

We recommend keeping a notebook with all relevant documentation easily accessible in the event you are asked to present it at military or police checkpoints.

Note that any boat over 14 feet in length is required to have a Temporary Boat Importation permit. Also know that every person present in a boat with fishing tackle is required to have a fishing license as well.

Traveling with Pets

Baja is a great place to travel with your pets. It's an even better place to find a pet to take home with you, and it's likely you'll come across many people with black mutts named "Baja" or one of the local beaches because there are so many strays.

When entering Mexico you will need to provide a current rabies vaccine record for each animal you are bringing with you. As with your vehicle registration, this record should show that the vaccine will be valid during the dates you list on your FMM for travel in Mexico.

Upon return to the US - with your original pet, or with any you may pick up along the way - you will again be asked to show rabies vaccination records.

Note that we have not been asked to show vaccine records when entering Mexico. But every US Customs and Border Patrol agent has asked for our paperwork upon returning to the US.

Drugs, Guns and Other Illegal Items

It should go without saying, but do not consider bringing drugs, guns or other illegal items into Mexico.

You should plan on having your vehicle thoroughly inspected upon arriving at INM at the border. And know that you will go through multiple military checkpoints as you travel through Baja and each one offers the opportunity for inspection.

Be aware that bullets, shell casings and even large knives will bring up more scrutiny than it is worth. And while the debate rages over whether marijuana is or is not legal within Mexico's border, it is not legal to carry it with you across the border.

Driving in Baja

Now that you have an idea about what it will take to get across the border, let's cover the topic of driving in Baja. No doubt you've come across horror stories on the internet, or perhaps from friends or family members, describing the dangers of driving in Baja.

And, generally speaking, driving in Baja can seem more dangerous than driving in other places in the world. But the reality is, if you follow several tips and remain aware of your surroundings you will find that even driving a large motorhome in Baja is not that difficult or dangerous.

Road Conditions & Speed Limits

Road conditions in Baja vary from incredibly smooth asphalt pavement along the southern portion of Federal Highway 5 to potholes, dirt, mud and soft sand in a variety of other places.

Generally speaking, the main highways (Federal Highway 1 and Federal Highway 5) are in pretty good condition for the length of the peninsula. However, various roads that offshoot to a variety of different smaller towns and villages and even within the towns themselves will be of questionable condition.

The biggest thing to consider about the road conditions in Baja is that there are very few places with any kind of meaningful shoulder. In fact, in many places, the highway is incredibly unforgiving and actually drops off just inches past the solid white line.

That said, it can be nerve-racking to drive on the highways in Baja, especially when you see semi-trucks approaching from either in front or behind you! The old adage, two hands on the wheel, applies. As does "slow and steady wins the race."

After all, you're there to enjoy Baja not to spend the entire time puckered up on the highway!

When it comes to indicating future road conditions, do not expect warnings as you may find in the US or Canada. There are several notoriously steep grades along the highway that are unmarked and likely over the double-digit legal limits you may be used to.

And our two favorite road signs, "Tope" (massive speed bump) and "Curvas Peligrosas" (dangerous curves) seem to be relative to whoever decided to put them there.

Speed limits in Baja reflect the road conditions relatively accurately. Limits are in kilometers per hour, so you may have to rely on the secondary km/hr markings on your speedometer or learn to do some quick math if you are not accustomed to the metric system.

There are a few areas where you will approach speeds of 65-70 mph, particularly in Baja California Sur as you near both La Paz and Cabo San Lucas from the north. But most of the time you will travel safely around 50-60 mph with little to no indication of when the speed limit drops drastically as you enter small villages and towns literally cut in half by the highway.

Additionally, we'll discuss "topes" in more detail in the section below. But these are speed bumps that you will encounter both on the highway and within cities and towns. They are quite effective at moderating speed and may take you by surprise from time to time.

Topes

A "tope" is a speed bump - real or imagined - that exists in a variety of shapes and forms and has been known to cause significant damage to RVs of all sorts. The reason we say "real or imagined" is that after a few hundred miles of driving over a dozen different kinds of topes, you'll find that sometimes a tope is just a painted strip across the highway designed to look like a speed bump.

Many of these will even have signs immediately in front of them indicating a tope. So you will slow down, as intended, and brace for the tope only to find it was not actually there. In other instances, there will be little to no warning before you hit the tope like Evel Knievel launching over a ramp!

Topes have been known to cause damage to RVs, particularly truck campers where the tie-downs have actually pulled free from the camper due to the rapid shock of the tope. Definitely be aware of what a tope is and how to recognize them when driving in Baja.

Expert Tip

We try not to be the first vehicle when it comes to driving in Baja. This is particularly true as we enter populated areas where things like topes, stop signs and roundabouts can be unexpected.

So we advise that you keep an eye out for other drivers ahead of you to know when a "real" tope is ahead. Locals know where the "fake" topes are located and will blaze through the painted stripes on the road accordingly.

But they also know where the real topes are, especially the large and annoying ones, and you will often see locals driving around the tope rather than over it.

Be mindful of these topes in particular as you'll see indications of vehicles that have bottomed out and scraped the top off the tope in the past.

Military Checkpoints

While many people like to criticize the presence of frequent military checkpoints in Baja, we consider them added protection against "the bad guys." Since we promote responsible travel and are never in possession of or in the act of doing anything illegal, we find they are mere temporary hindrances to getting from one place to another.

Still, others have horror stories they like to share on social media about how they were set up or stolen from at a military checkpoint.

The reality is, the Mexican government utilizes military checkpoints manned by local, state and federal police and military officers to keep crime in check. Although they are primarily interested in suspicious vehicles smuggling illegal drugs, weapons and/ or humans, military checkpoints will occasionally find recreational travelers guilty of breaking the law, particularly when it comes to possession of marijuana.

We have experienced a range of activity and behavior at various checkpoints throughout our time in traveling Baja and none have breached what we would consider ordinary and customary protocol.

However, there are stories out there of travelers who had bad experiences. We encourage safe, responsible travel everywhere you may go and when traveling in Baja, be safe and responsible as you approach each military checkpoint

Expert Tip

Do NOT attempt to bribe officers at military checkpoints. An unspoken custom among many seasonal travelers in Baja is to bring snacks and small gifts for the officers, particularly around Christmas.

While it may be a kind gesture (and we are all about promoting kind gestures in the world!), giving gifts such as these creates a subculture of expectation among some officers where they expect every RV to offer them something.

In the event you happen to have a more expectant officer inspect your vehicle, the lack of a "gift" may result in instances some have come to call bribes.

For this reason it is better for everyone if you simply do as you are expected to do at each military checkpoint: stop the vehicle, answer any questions to the best of your ability, offer your passport and FMM as required, allow for an inspection of your vehicle if requested, smile and drive on.

and we suspect the best parts of human nature will prevail more times than not.

Driving after Dark

The number 1 rule for driving in Baja is "do not drive at night." The number 2 rule for driving in Baja is "do not drive at night."

There are a number of reasons why it is best not to drive at night. And yes, on several occasions we have found ourselves racing the sunset to get to our next campsite. But as a general principle, do not drive at night unless you have to.

Here are a few reasons why:

Reasons Not to Drive at Night

1. Cows (and horses) will migrate to eat along the highway in the evening hours. You'll see cow carcasses every few miles indicating how frequently they are hit by passing vehicles.
2. You can also note the size of many semi truck brush guards as another indicator of the expectation truck drivers have of literally running into a cow in the middle of the night. This is an unnecessary risk for someone on an adventure exploring Baja. Plan your trips accordingly and limit your night drives.
3. Road hazards are harder to see at night. Sometimes it is near impossible to see where the shoulder disappears, the potholes occur or the tope jumps out of nowhere even in the middle of the day.
4. And judging which tracks to follow down a sandy road is challenging enough. Imagine trying to navigate such hazards in the dark!
5. Emergency services and help are fewer and further between. Green Angles (discussed below) do travel the main highways at a regular frequency to assist drivers in need. But it is more dangerous to be broken down during the night, particularly when there are no shoulders or safe areas to pull over.

Green Angels

Green Angels are government employees that patrol the main highways throughout Baja. They are bilingual mechanics capable of assisting in most roadside emergencies. Green Angels will do everything from providing mechanical assistance and medical first aid to towing your vehicle, if possible.

This is a great service offered to all travelers in Baja because it means that you will have assistance at some point even if the worst thing happens during your drive. There are phenomenal stories out there of everyday people helping each other out in the midst of breakdowns and accidents along the highway.

But in the event you break down, have a flat tire or are in need of other services, it is good to know that the Green Angeles are never too far away.

Offroad Driving

Baja is renowned for its rugged offroad terrain. In fact, the famous Baja offroad races (Baja 1000 and Baja 500 among them) have grown in popularity each year from the challenge that offroad driving in Baja provides.

But even if you're not driving in the Baja 1000, or driving out to a remote place to watch the race, it is good to know that there are tons of roads you can take offroad — whether in your primary vehicle or in a separate ATV or dirt bike.

Expert Tip

We suggest that you have the following tools and equipment on hand when traveling in Baja to aid yourself and others in need:

- Portable air compressor
- Recovery traction pads
- Shovel
- Wood blocks/RV leveling blocks
- Jack & full-size mounted spare tire

In some cases, offroad driving is the ONLY driving if you want to reach places like Agua Verde in Baja California Sur or some of the surf breaks around Scorpion Bay (San Juanico).

Regardless of whether you're looking for the ultimate offroad adventure, or simply have to drive a few miles of washboard road to reach a quiet, isolated camping spot for a few nights, exercise caution and do be prepared with proper safety and tools, including recovery gear.

Although we've assisted more people stuck offroad than the times we've been assisted, it is an unspoken principle that you are very likely to find yourself stuck somewhere. Keep calm, work the solution and accept any help that comes your way!

Tips for Driving In Baja

Although you can likely pull the most important Baja driving tips from the previous sections, we thought it was important to include our top suggestions in a place that stands out.

Here are our top tips for driving in Baja:

Baja Driving Tips

- Don't drive at night unnecessarily. And be even more alert for wildlife in the twilight hours.
- Drive the speed limit. Take your time and enjoy the scenery while being safe.
- Stop (fully!) at stop signs, even if other drivers are not. You are a target for police in an RV.
- Heed the safety signs. (But know they aren't always accurate!)
- Tuck in and adjust your side-view mirrors so they stick out as little as possible.
- Know that semi trucks will more often turn their left turn signal on to let you know when it is safe to pass than to actually turn left.
- Don't pay the bribe. There is almost always an open police office or special traffic court where you can follow the police officer to pay traffic citations in person.

Staying Safe and Healthy in Baja

If the concern that other people have for you over crossing the border and driving in Baja isn't enough, it's likely that you'll hear plenty of people warn you about staying safe and healthy in Baja.

And while there are sporadic incidents and pockets of violence in Baja just like anywhere else in the world, generally speaking, you are safer in Baja than you are in many US metropolitan areas.

We don't believe in jinxes or the power of knocking on wood. But we do believe that doing right, treating others with kindness (especially when we are guests in their country) and avoiding generally unsafe situations will go a long, long way to improving your safety and health while traveling in Baja.

Aside from a little petty theft here and there (old shoes, an empty propane tank, a half-full container of drinking water), we have not experienced any major crime in all the time we have spent in Baja.

The Mexican people are incredibly welcoming and hospitable and most know that it is bad for business for crime to affect tourists. In fact, we've learned stories in the past of how locals have policed their own neighborhoods and have taken things into their own hands to hold thieves responsible for crimes against tourists.

And we have had significant health issues arise while traveling in Baja that has led us to seek emergency medical assistance, both for ourselves and for our dogs.

So it is good to know that there are ways of staying safe and healthy when traveling in Baja. And we'll cover the big topics in the following sections.

Health, Hospitals & Pharmacies

Not only are most clinics and hospitals in Baja comparable to those in the US, but also many are above the US standard and offer services at a fraction of the cost. Border cities in particular have taken advantage of US-trained medical and dental professionals to create "medical tourism" opportunities where Americans and Canadians will actually plan trips to Baja just to seek medical attention.

Whether having root canals and fillings done or seeking alternative cancer treatments not authorized north of the border, travelers have come to expect quality and expertise in healthcare in Baja.

Additionally, pharmacies are also top-notch and offer everything you could expect to find in your local pharmacy with a few additions you may not have access to back home. Know that pharmacies do have limits and safety protocols in place for controlled substances similar to in the US and Canada.

But you can also find partnering clinics to assist in diagnosing and prescribing virtually any medication you may want or need.

A note on prescriptions: If you have prescriptions that you take be sure to account for having enough medicine to last the duration of your trip. While you may be able to find a doctor able to prescribe new medication, we find it is always easier to carry plenty with us. Do be sure to leave it in the original prescription bottle in the event that you are inspected and the officer asks about it.

Expert Tip

If you plan to stay in an area for any extended amount of time, ask the locals or connect with ex-pat groups on social media to determine where they go for medical treatment.

You never want to plan an illness or accident. But in the event you need medical assistance, it is good to have a phone number and/or address within reach to ensure you have the best care you can receive as promptly as possible.

We take a large number of daily vitamins and supplements. And when you multiply that out over 4-5 months, it means we carry lots of bottles.

Every time we crossed the border and were inspected we were asked about the nature of the containers. Each time we were able to explain and relate what they were and why we needed them.

Food and Drinking Water

Everybody knows that you "don't drink the water in Mexico." But what you may not know is that there are abundant "aqua purificados" (purified water dispensaries) in virtually every town throughout Baja. Most are equipped to be able to fill your RV or van tank with reverse osmosis purified water.

But at the least you can fill five-gallon "garrafones" for virtually nothing. Drinking only from agua purificados and sealed water bottles purchased in the store is the best way to ensure that you do not become ill with any water-borne disease.

When it comes to food, there are a few things to know. Most reputable restaurants will use purified water to rinse their vegetables and other foods.

Expert Tip

We always carry extra fresh water drinking containers specifically for purified water. If you have the space, we'd encourage you to consider having dedicated drinking water containers above and beyond any fresh water tank space you may have.

This will be beneficial particularly if you plan on perfecting the art of boondocking in Baja, for which the opportunity is ripe.

Business owners understand that if a handful of tourists get sick, word will get out (particularly on social media) and the tourist business will dry up. So it is worth the few extra pesos for these places to rinse their food properly in purified water.

In other instances, you will want to be aware of food that has been left to sit out all day. When we purchase fresh seafood and meat from local vendors we do so first thing in the morning when they have their freshest offerings. We also wash our vegetables with a vinegar water solution.

Safety & Security

Baja is generally as safe as anywhere else in North America. But there are always isolated instances and situations where safety and security should be at the forefront of your mind. The best practice is always to be aware of your surroundings.

Whether you are driving, parking or walking around, be mindful of the people around you. All cities in Baja have the same safety threats as cities anywhere else in the world.

There may be rare instances of petty theft and vandalism. But these are few and far between, especially when targeted at tourists.

Outside of the metro areas, where you will likely spend most of your time, there is very little risk of any kind. Many of the smaller towns use a sort of self-governance when it comes to preventing and punishing localized crime.

There are stories of thefts of bikes and other small property from campgrounds where the items were quickly returned because community members knew exactly who took the items. Rarely does crime escalate beyond this.

But do use some common sense when it comes to where you drive, park and camp. There are "bad parts" of towns and cities where there exists more opportunity for crime, likely just the same as back home. You'll quickly see the signs that you may want to keep moving - though unless you are in a border city where crime is more prevalent, these are not very common.

Note that when it comes to picking out a camping spot for the night we do NOT advocate for "stealth camping" in places that are not specifically designated as either formal or informal campsites. There are places where people have pulled over behind a restaurant or business to sleep for the night that invite the possibility of trouble.

If you stick with the beaten path when it comes to selecting your camping areas you will likely have no incidents. Do not let this discourage you from wandering off the beaten path a bit to find your private, secluded beach spot if that is what you are after. But know that there is always safety in numbers and in following the general herd when it comes to camping.

And whether you are camping alone or with a group, we've found that having motion sensor lights is a great way to discourage any theft around the campsite. There are lots of great options for portable solar powered and battery-operated motion sensor lights that you do not need to permanently mount or wire to your RV.

Expert Tip

When camping in more remote places, keep in mind when and where you have cell reception. The cellular network across Baja is expanding quickly each year. But there are many "dead zones" where you may not have service.

In the event of an emergency, it is always good practice to remember about when/where you last had service so you can call for help.

CHAPTER 2

Camping Logistics in Baja

Now that we've covered the basics about planning for what life is like in and around Baja, it's time to cover specific logistics for camping and living in Baja.

In this chapter, we'll help you understand just how easy and affordable it is to spend a few weeks or months traveling through the beautiful Baja peninsula.

Conversions (KM/Mile, Liter/Gal, Peso/USD)

One of the first things you should notice when crossing the border is that you may have to learn how to do a few simple conversions during your time in Baja. If you're coming from Canada, most of these will be familiar to you already.

But coming from the US, you'll want to be able to understand and compute the following conversions.

- **Kilometer/Mile** - There are 0.621371 miles in a kilometer. So when it comes to calculating distances or speed limits, you can take the posted kilometer amount and multiple by 0.621371 (or just round to 0.62 or 0.6) to determine the more familiar miles.

> **For example:**
> - 80 km/h speed limit is 80 km/h x 0.62 = 49.6 mph
> - 100 km distance = 100 km x 0.62 = 62 miles

- **Liters/Gallons** - There are 3.78541 liters in a gallon. So if you want to calculate how much fuel you are adding to your tank, you can divide the total number of liters by 3.78541 (or just round to 3.8) to determine the more familiar gallons.

> **For example:**
> - 100 liters / 3.8 = 26.3 gallons

- **Pesos/USD/CAD** - This will depend on the exchange rates between Mexican and US/Canadian currency. Generally, there are around 20 pesos to the US dollar and 15 pesos to the Canadian dollar. But you will want to confirm the exchange rate at and during the time of travel.

Cash, Credit Cards and ATMs

Baja used to be an entirely cash-based economy. Everything from taco stands to gas stations required payment in pesos (or sometimes US dollars).

Now there are far more places that accept credit cards - though it is important to note that you should not expect all vendors to accept credit cards.

Cash is still king in Baja. But getting cash from an ATM can be a bit frustrating and costly, depending on where you are, what bank ATM you use and what your home bank is.

We have found that a general principle for taking money out of an ATM is that you will receive more favorable exchange rates and lower fees the further you are from the border and outside of smaller towns.

For example, our favorite town in Baja only has one ATM in town. As such, there are strict limits on how much money you can withdraw at one time. Not only does this seem to change from week to week, but also the ATM was known to run out of money quite frequently.

Further, exchange rates were not favorable, often around 7-10% less than what it should be AND the ATM fees were around $8 USD whether you were taking out $20 or $400 USD in pesos.

On the other hand, when you walk into WalMart or Soriana (a large chain grocery store) in La Paz you will be greeted by a wall of 3 or 4 different ATMs from which to choose. The exchange rate for each is similar and nearly the posted rate for the day.

And the ATM fees were around $2 USD per transaction with much higher daily limits. They were never out of money and, depending on your bank's daily limits, you could go from one ATM to the next to withdraw cash if you needed.

Expert Tip

We have both a Capital One and Charles Schwab checking account for our international travel. Capital One offers competitive exchange rates at ATMs and with credit card purchases with no additional foreign transaction fees.

However, it does not reimburse the ATM fees incurred at the ATM. On the other hand, Charles Schwab offers comparable rates with no foreign transaction fees AND they reimburse the ATM fees at the end of each month. After years of international travel we find that Charles Schwab is the best overall bank for travelers.

We use Capital One to purchase fuel, groceries, tours and other big-ticket items when possible and Charles Schwab for taking out cash at ATMs.

Contact us directly if you are interested in opening a Capital One account. We'll send you a link where you can quickly open an account and credit card with a $200 cash bonus!

Check with your bank before you travel to Baja to confirm any special conditions, rates or fees associated with using your debit and/or credit cards in Mexico.

We found that the bank we use for our daily needs in the US, one of the biggest national banks in the US, offers very unfavorable exchange rates and tacks on "foreign transaction fees" whether you spend $1 or $1,000 USD.

Knowing this in advance has saved us hundreds, if not thousands, of dollars in unnecessary fees because we found a different bank to use when we travel in Baja.

Fresh Water for your RV Tank

Regardless of the age of our fresh water tank and how often we give it a deep clean, we do not drink the water from our fresh water tank - whether in Mexico, Canada or the US. However, we do ensure that we have the highest quality water in our fresh water tank as we use this water for cooking and bathing.

Water for your RV fresh water tanks is in abundance all throughout Baja. As we recommend that you visit "agua purificados" for drinking water, most of these purified water stations offer a "manguera" or hose for you to be able to fill up your RV tank.

Most agua purificados meter their dispenser and you will find they can top you off in no time at all. Purified water is incredibly affordable and we recommend that you plan to visit these for your water refills as often as possible due to the quality of the water you will receive.

Note, however, that some aguas purificados do not have hoses and/or meters. And for these, you may have to get creative with using smaller containers or several types of hose adapters to transfer water into your tank.

As an alternative to aguas purificados, you will find lots of places throughout Baja that have traditional water spigots from which you may ask permission to fill your water tank.

Nearly all campgrounds, even those only offering dry camping, have water spigots. And you can ask many businesses and even private residences (only in a true bind) if you may fill up with water.

Most people in Baja will be very helpful and remember to always offer a fair amount of pesos in exchange for their water.

When it comes to ensuring the water is safe for consumption, you can trust agua purificados to provide high-quality drinking water. These businesses exist not for the RVers who flock to Baja each winter, but rather for local residents who rely on purified water over tap water.

Expert Tip

We carry a variety of hose/pipe adapters and fittings, particularly the "Water Bandit," as a way to hedge our bets when it comes to filling up our water tanks. The Water Bandit will allow you to connect your fresh water hose to virtually any spigot.

Of course, explaining its use to someone unfamiliar with how it works may be a challenge. But having a Water Bandit vastly increases your opportunity for locating water in Baja.

But if you cannot find an agua purificado, it is perfectly fine to add a little liquid bleach to your water tank to purify the water in the tank. You should use approximately 2 teaspoons for every 10 gallons of water in your tank.

We recommend that you try to alternate between adding water and adding bleach to your tank so that it mixes as you fill. However, driving around Baja for any amount of time is sure to mix the bleach and water adequately prior to using.

Sewer / Dump Stations

Although there are not as many dump stations in Baja as you may find in the US and Canada, there are plenty of them spaced out in intervals that make it quite easy to plan your trips to dump your black and grey tanks. The most reliable places for dumping your wastewater tanks will be campgrounds.

Sewage facilities range from rudimentary septic systems to highly complex ones that filter, process and recycle wastewater. Regardless of their complexity, dump stations are convenient and located all throughout Baja primarily in more highly populated cities and towns.

Most campgrounds offer sewer hookups, which makes it quite easy to ensure that every time you stay at a campground you can empty your tanks before leaving. Even if you do not stay in the campground, many will allow you to dump your sewage for a small fee.

When we camp at the beaches around La Paz, for instance, we almost always make a frequent trip to Campestre La Maranatha to empty our tanks (and do our laundry!).

Expert Tip

We recommend that you empty your tanks every time you stay at a campground with sewer facilities. Although we enjoy boondocking as much as the next person, we still add a night in a campground here or there if only to empty our tanks, fill up on water and grab a little less-limited hot water shower.

It is also good practice to gauge how often you need to empty your tanks - whether you trust your tank gauges or not.

LPG / Propane Refills

Although not as abundant as purified drinking water, propane is widely available in most larger towns and cities throughout Baja.

Whether you have portable propane cylinders that you can remove and take for a refill or have permanently mounted cylinders that require you to drive your RV to the propane center, you will have no issues keeping your propane cylinders topped off while in Baja.

Expert Tip

Like most consumption when it comes to RVs, we recommend that you have a general idea of how quickly or slowly you exhaust your propane tank(s). While propane can be found in most population centers, sometimes it is not always convenient to access.

So having an idea of how pressing your refill is will better help you make the decision as to which facility to visit. For example, there is a very easily accessible propane refill facility on the north end of Santa Rosalia and another one on the south end of Loreto.

However, refilling propane in Mulege, which is right between these towns, is quite difficult. So we recommend that you budget your propane use such that you can consider refilling in either Santa Rosalia or Loreto.

We also recommend that you consider adding an "Extend A Stay" device to your vehicle propane tank. This will allow you to use portable external tanks to feed your propane appliances as well as to use your vehicle tank to provide fuel for your outdoor grill or fire pit.

Having the ability to use portable propane tanks may make extending your stay in some places more convenient because it may be easier to refill a portable tank than to have to find a place to refill your RV propane tank.

There are a few companies that offer both drive-up and portable cylinder servicing throughout the peninsula. The two that you will see the most are Gaspasa and Baja Gas.

Most propane refill facilities will offer both options. However, do note that some will not. In La Paz, for example, there is one dedicated portable refill facility and several facilities that you can drive up to.

Fuel

Fuel, both regular gasoline and diesel, is abundantly available throughout Baja. There are only a few stretches of highway, particularly along a 200-mile (320 km) stretch of Federal Highway 1 between El Rosario on the north and Jesus Maria to the south, where fuel is limited.

And even here it is possible to purchase fuel from 55-gallon drums from vendors on the side of the road (if you trust the quality!). Virtually everywhere else throughout Baja should be within your fuel tank range. However, we like to try and stay above half a tank as we travel the peninsula out of an abundance of caution.

When it comes to filling your fuel tank, do not expect to pump your own gas. In fact, all gas stations in Baja will have pump attendants that will take care of that for you. Although there have been many rumors of deceitful activities at various gas stations in Baja over the years, you are likely to have a positive experience, particularly if you follow these procedures.

First, pull up to the pump completely before stopping your vehicle. Use your side-view mirror to keep an eye on the attendant, who will likely advise you when it is OK to stop. Then, immediately get out of your vehicle to meet the attendant at the pump.

You can sort through your wallet and other items in the RV once the pump is turned on. But it is important to greet the attendant before they begin pumping fuel.

The attendant will ask you what type of fuel you would like and then they will "zero out" the meter. Good attendants are use to skeptical tourists looking over their shoulders and they will show you the zeros ("ceros") on their own initiative.

If the attendant does not show you the zeros, ask them kindly. This is one way in which past scams have taken place, whereby you overpay for gas you do not receive because the pump already shows some amount on the screen.

When it comes time to pay, if paying with cash, be sure to count the bills out in plain sight. Another rumored scam is unsavory attendants claiming either that you did not hand them the proper amount of cash or that they hand you back a wad of change that is not properly counted.

Expert Tip

Using a cashback or points-based credit card is a good way to take advantage of being able to use your preferred credit card at most gas stations in Baja. However, it is also good practice to always have pesos on hand (US dollars as a last resort) in the event you are unable to use your credit card at the only gas station around.

For example, there is still a cash-only gas station in the Bay of Los Angeles where we have known several travelers to get creative in payment as they were nearly 100 miles (160 km) from the next closest gas station.

We use our Capital One Cashback Credit card to receive unlimited 1.5% cashback on all fuel payments with zero foreign transaction fees.

Contact us directly if you are interested in opening a Capital One account. We'll send you a link where you can quickly open an account and credit card with a $200 cash bonus.

When paying with cash, we always hand over near exact amounts and count it out as we hand it to the attendant. It is very likely they will still recount it in front of you. However, having exact or close to exact change will make it less likely you will have any negative experience when getting fuel.

And yes, we recommend that you follow this procedure every time you get fuel. We trust people quite a bit. But it is wise to always be aware as this issue with gas station attendants in particular has drawn the ire of many travelers over the years.

Note, it is not required or customary to tip the attendant. However, we will typically round up a few pesos when paying with cash as a simple gesture of gratitude to someone who works all day for very little pay.

Groceries

Although smaller towns and villages will have mostly localized grocery stores, there are very few items you will not be able to find in one fashion or another.

Larger metropolitan areas such as Tijuana, Mexicali, Ensenada, La Paz and Cabo San Lucas have larger grocery chains with a much wider selection of products. You'll even find Costco, Sam's Club and WalMart in these places.

Even in popular tourist destinations like Loreto, Los Barriles and Todos Santos you'll find smaller grocery stores that carry many of the name-brand products that you will recognize from home.

However, if you have a specialized diet or certain dietary restrictions we would advise you to stock up prior to entering Baja.

Expert Tip

We always stock up at our favorite grocery store before crossing the border into Mexico. Sometimes this feels gluttonous until we use the last of whatever item we packed and find ourselves missing the next serving.

Clearly how much you pack depends on your personal preferences and how long you will be traveling in Baja. However, certain dietary restrictions will be difficult to accommodate so if it is a matter of allergies or discomfort, consider stocking up.

We also have a secondary portable 12-volt freezer we use to store high-quality meat we purchase in the US prior to visiting Baja as it is virtually impossible to find grass-fed and free range meats.

Cellular Service/Wifi in Baja

Cellular service and WiFi availability in Baja have drastically improved year over year. However, there are definite stretches of "dead zones" where you can expect to be without cellular service. In fact, finding these areas is still a joy to many travelers looking to travel to Baja to disconnect from the world to take in many of the off-the-beaten-path adventures that still exist on the rugged peninsula.

The days of having to purchase daily international plans or relying on local SIM cards are all but past when you travel to Baja. Most major US carriers and many Canadian carriers provide service when you travel to Mexico. However, it is up to you to discuss with your carrier any restrictions, fees or other limitations on your cellular plan.

Throughout Baja, you will see TelCel as the major Mexican cellular carrier. The major US carriers will use TelCel towers to provide service based on your plan. So do not be surprised when you see TelCel pop up in your phone settings.

If you do not have a cellular plan that includes Mexico in its coverage, an alternative is to purchase a TelCel SIM card from any number of TelCel retailers. There are official TelCel stores that are trustworthy to assist you in this matter.

However, you can also find TelCel distributors at any number of corner stores, such as OXXO, that can also provide you with a SIM card.

Expert Tip

TelCel has had an unlimited 2-hour packet you can purchase for under $1 (around 15 pesos at time of writing). This is by far the least expensive packet and you can use multiple unlimited packets back to back throughout the day, especially if you need to put together an 8-hour mobile work day.

However, you must have a balance in your Amigo account and you will want to set an alarm to remind yourself when it is time to renew the unlimited packet. If the unlimited packet lapses, TelCel will charge your account at the highest data rate possible and you will quickly find your balance depleted.

Activating the SIM card and accessing cellular service may be a little tricky, depending on how well you can understand Spanish. For this reason, we advise you try an official TelCel store and ask politely if anyone can assist you in English.

Regardless of whether you need a SIM card for cellular service or not, we always travel with a TelCel SIM card to access the best WiFi you will find in Baja.

Although WiFi is offered at various campgrounds, restaurants and other public places, we have found that using the TelCel cellular network via a local SIM card provides the most reliable WiFi if you need to stay connected.

You will need an activated TelCel SIM card to create an online account either through the mobile app or website. Once you create an online registration you can fund what is called your "Amigo" account either by paying cash at a TelCel distributor or by using your credit card.

With funding in your account, you can select any of a number of "paquetes" ("packet") that provide various quantities of data. Use your mobile device to broadcast a hot spot and you will have WiFi for all of your devices.

A note on Starlink: Starlink for RVers is now available and more and more campers are taking advantage of being able to use their Starlink satellite dish virtually anywhere they travel. We have Starlink as well and appreciate the connectivity, albeit at a $135 USD per month premium!

However, be aware that as of the time of writing, Starlink's official policy on using Starlink outside of your country of residence is that you can only expect 2 months of service before having to return to your home country or purchasing a Starlink in the new country.

Some users have equated this to highway robbery and there is a discussion about workarounds. We cannot speak to either and encourage you to play by the rules and/or do your own research on whether Starlink will make a better option for you during your time in Baja.

Ferries

If you are interested in taking a ferry to the mainland there are several options through Baja Ferry. The most popular option is to take the ferry from La Paz to either Mazatlan or Topolobampa from the Pichilingue ferry terminal.

However, there is also an option to ferry from Santa Rosalia to Guaymas. But this is less popular and less reliable.

To ferry to the mainland you will be required to have a Mexican Temporary Importation Permit for your vehicle, valid Mexican auto insurance and your FMM.

If you are considering taking the ferry to the mainland it is best to obtain your TIP at the time you cross the border. There are special forms you will need to complete in addition to a nominal deposit, which will be returned to you upon your departure from Mexico.

Note that you are not required to have a TIP when traveling in Baja, so this is often overlooked by travelers when crossing the border. If you have any inclination of taking the ferry to the mainland, be sure to purchase your TIP in advance. You can actually apply for the TIP up to 60 days in advance of your arrival in Baja.

- For more information on the ferry service and fees be sure to visit the Baja Ferry website.
- For more information on obtaining a TIP be sure to visit the Banjercito website.

Traveling with Dogs/Pets

Mexico is very pet-friendly when it comes to traveling with your furry family members. There are no quarantine procedures or expensive costs involved in crossing the border with your pet.

However, you will need to have up-to-date medical records for your pets - particularly the rabbies vaccine.

Although it is up to the border agent whether or not you will be asked to present current vaccination documentation, it is best practice to keep all of your pets' medical records together for quick access. It is very unlikely that you will have to present this paperwork once you have passed through Mexican customs and are traveling through Baja.

RVING BAJA

However, US Customs and Border Protection is all but guaranteed to check your paperwork upon your return to the US. So be sure that your pets vaccination status is valid all the way through your return.

Veterinarians in Baja are incredible and offer the same quality experience you would expect back home at a fraction of the cost. So if your pet needs medical attention or updated shots, or if you pick up an additional pet in Baja to bring home with you, it is relatively easy and inexpensive to bring their medical records up to date.

We have had the unfortunate need to visit several vets each time we have visited Baja and we were always incredibly thankful for the high level of professionalism and treatment our pets received.

Returning to the US

Returning to the US is virtually the same process, but in reverse, as crossing into Mexico. If you are a US citizen, you will be required to present your passport, vehicle registration and pet records.

You may find that your vehicle will go through an xray machine and/ or you might be asked to go through a secondary inspection where customs agents will go through your entire RV.

Note, US Customs and Border Patrol agents have not cared whether or not we included the FMM in our paperwork to return to the US. But it is still important to keep your FMM on hand until you cross back into the US.

CHAPTER 3

Where to Go in Baja California

We have divided this chapter about places to visit in the northern state of Baja California into 2 sections based on the geography of the peninsula.

The first section will address destinations on the west coast, or Pacific Ocean, side of the state. This will cover locations mostly found off Federal Highway 1 along the ocean.

The second section will address destinations on the east coast, or Sea of Cortez, side of the state. This will cover locations mostly found off Federal Highway 5 along the sea.

Both sections will cover Baja California from north to south as though you were traveling into the peninsula from the US border on either highway.

Destinations Along Federal Highway 1

Federal Highway 1 runs the length of the Baja peninsula from Tijuana to Cabo San Lucas. In Baja California there are numerous places worth spending a few days to a few weeks visiting.

From the wine country of Valle de Guadalupe to smaller fishing and farming communities along the Pacific Ocean, these are our top recommended places to consider visiting as you explore Baja.

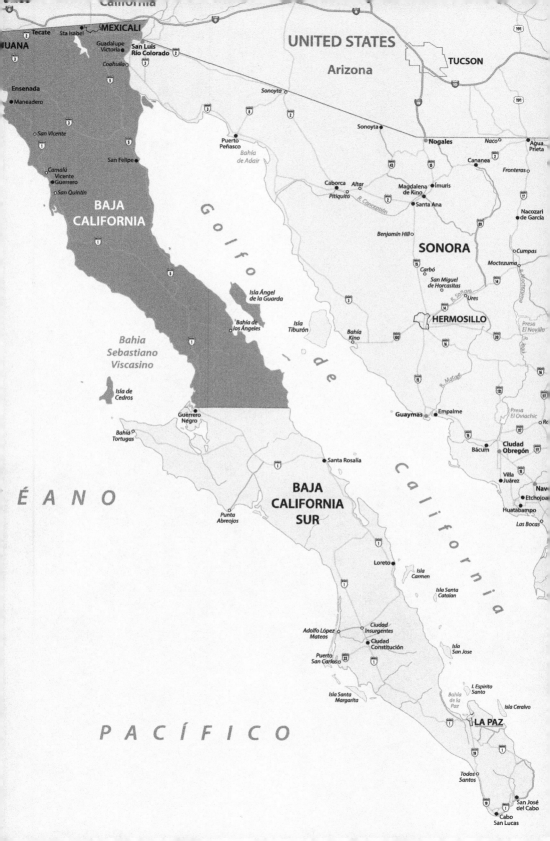

Valle de Guadalupe

Valle De Guadalupe is the premier wine region of Mexico with over ⅔ of the wine in the country sourced here. Just 45 miles (70 km) from Tecate or 70 miles (110 km) from Tijuana, the area is easily accessible for travelers of all sorts.

The culinary exploration, beautiful resorts, fine dining restaurants, and wineries have grabbed global attention and made this part of Baja a must-visit for anyone interested in splurging a little.

In fact, if you do not have much time to visit Baja or just want to make a long weekend to get your feet wet on the Baja experience, Valle de Guadalupe is a comfortable first stop.

Situated inland around 30 miles (45 km) northeast of Ensenada, Valle de Guadalupe is easily accessible from Tecate, Tijuana or Ensenada making it one of the more popular places to visit in Baja California.

The Spanish first planted grapes in the region in the 16th century and since then many communities and winemaking pioneers have put their mark on the valley. The 1000-foot elevation above sea level and Mediterranean microclimate creates a perfect environment for growing a variety of grapes.

Some popular Mexican wine varieties you can find here are Zinfandel, Cabernet Sauvignon, Carignan, Merlot, Malbec, Nebbiolo for the red, and Chenin Blanc, Muscat Blanc, Riesling, and Sauvignon Blanc.

The fine restaurants, wineries, and lodges are open throughout the year. But the valley comes to life in summer when seasonal restaurants open to serve the best food with the views of stunning vineyards and valleys.

Moreover, October is also quite popular because of Valle Food & Wine Festival where the finest Michelin star chefs and wineries serve the best meals made from locally grown ingredients.

Things to Do in Valle de Guadalupe

There are many things to do in Valle De Guadalupe, including visiting numerous restaurants, wineries, vineyards, outdoor activities, and beautiful sceneries. Here are a few of the top things to consider when visiting Valle De Guadalupe.

Check out all the Wineries

You cannot visit Valle de Guadalupe without touring the wineries. There are over 25 wineries, and each has something different to offer.

You can do a self-guided tour stopping at whichever vineyards suit your interests. Or join a formal tour and take the stress of driving and parking away.

Some popular wineries in the valley are:

- Vinisterrs
- Don Tomas Vinedo
- Nativo
- Vena Cava
- Monte Xanic
- Xecue
- Casa Magoni

Discover the Food

Food and wine are like horse and carriage in Valle de Guadalupe. Whether you dine at your favorite vineyard or seek out an established restaurant, you'll be greeted with one of the best culinary experiences Baja has to offer at one of over 30 established restaurants.

These are some of the top restaurants that you should consider during your visit:

- Animalon
- Cassa Frida
- Fauna
- Deckman's en el Mogor
- Finca Altozano

Attend the Annual Festivals

Valle de Guadalupe really comes to life in summer. Multiple festivals are held throughout August, September, and October to showcase the region and the valley's rich wine and food culture.

You may want to plan your trip according to the festival dates:

- Ruta del Vino – Annual bicycle road race festival held in July
- Harvest Festival – August 5th
- Arroces y Vino – August 12th
- Paellas Festival – August 21st
- El Valle Music Festival – September 3rd
- Valle Food and Wine Festival – in the first 10 days of October

Learn about the History

There are a few museums in Valle de Guadalupe, which is a great way to learn about the wine-producing area of Mexico. Two of the most important museums of Guadalupe are:

- **Wine and Vine Museum** – Located on the Ruta Del Vino showcases the culture, history, industry, art, wine, and identity of the valley. The museum has a great 360 view of vineyards and surrounding mountains around the valley.
- **Museo Historico Comunitario** – A small and enjoyable place with many informative collections about the Kumiai Culture of

the region and Russian influence on the Valle de Guadalupe and wine production.

Splurge on a Spa and Massage Day

After touring wineries and museums, it is time to take the load off the muscles with a massage and spa treatment. There are many spa options in Valle de Guadalupe.

You can either go to Viniphera, arguably the best spa in Valle de Guadalupe. Or just book a Valle mobile massage and have a masseuse come to you at your campground or hotel.

Campgrounds in Valle de Guadalupe

Although there are not a lot of options for camping in Valle de Guadalupe, the options available will provide all the amenities you could want or need if you're planning to enjoy your time in the valley.

El Valle RV Park

Address:	Rancho San Marcos s/n El Porvenir, 22750 Francisco Zarco (Valle de Guadalupe), B.C., Mexico
Website:	http://elvallervpark.com/
Phone Number:	+52 646 276 1494
GPS Coordinates:	32.0195, -116.6689
Price Range:	$20 - 40 USD

El Valle RV Park is an excellent campground that includes campsites, cozy barrel pods, giant 30ft silver wine bottle, and RV sites. El Valle has a perfect location surrounded by beautiful green mountains and has all the amenities and luxury you need to stay peacefully.

Plus, it is within walking distance to La Cocina de Dona Esthela, a small restaurant made famous by being a top pick of Anthony Bordain and a must-visit if you camp here.

Guadalupe RV Park

Website: https://guadalupepark.com/

Phone Number: +52 646 171 1770

GPS Coordinates: 32.1119, -116.5469

Price Range: $20+ USD

Guadalupe RV Park is another excellent campground in Valle de Guadalupe. The campground is just minutes away from the hustle of the town and popular tourist spots. It is big rig friendly and has all the facilities to entertain around 30 RVs at once.

Ensenada

Ensenada, located on the Northwestern end of the peninsula, is the third-largest city in Baja California. The coastal city is built around Todos Santos Bay on the Pacific Ocean and is about 90 miles (140 km) south of San Diego.

Ensenada is a major tourist destination because of its temperate Mediterranean climate, beaches, food, water sports, and excellent nightlife.

The city itself has a population of around half a million people and is surrounded by beautiful beaches and mountains that attract many more people throughout the year. The Port of Ensenada is the only deep-water port in the region creating a thriving economic hub that links Mexico with many countries around the world. Moreover, the port also welcomes more than 200 cruise ships per year.

In addition to trade importance, the coast has been a sanctuary for gray whales, white sharks, sea lions, and hundreds of other species. Coyotes, bobcats, pumas and various other land animals are also abundant in the area.

Ensenada has a mild climate with only a little annual rain, creating an excellent environment for wheat, grapes, and olives to grow throughout the nearby Valle de Guadalupe.

The mild climate also makes it a popular spot for tourists throughout the year. The city has exceptional resorts, hotels, vacation homes, and condos spread along the northern and southern shores.

Ensenada has something for everyone - from watersports, beach sports and fishing activities to top-rated restaurants, mouthwatering seafood, taco stands, spas, and museums. Moreover, it is just 45-minute away from the Mexican wine county of Valle de Guadalupe, where you can see some of the finest wineries in the world.

Whether you are visiting for a day or planning a weekend escape, the activities will keep you amused throughout your journey.

Things to Do in Ensenada

Although Ensenada is quite a bit larger than most other cities and towns in Baja, it still holds the charm of a small town.

Here are the things to do in Ensenada.

Experience La Bufadora

La Bufadora is among the favorite tourist spots in Ensenada. It is a natural marine geyser located just 45 minutes along a scenic drive from the city center. As one of the biggest blowholes in the world, La Bufadora can push water through its spout over 50 feet every few seconds.

The best time to visit La Bufadora is during the high tide to ensure that you are witnessing the marine geyser in its full glory.

Eat Delicious Seafood

Ensenada has been known to serve some of the best seafood in all of Mexico. It is the home to world-famous fish tacos and has supreme street food stalls that sell food at incredibly reasonable prices.

Depending on how long you plan to spend in Ensenada, you can taste authentic Mexican food such as tostadas, fish tacos, clams, carne asada, shrimp and much more at a variety of restaurants throughout the city.

Some of the best Seafood restaurants in Ensenada are:

- Tacos Lily (fish tacos)
- Mercado Negro (seafood market and restaurants)
- Mariscos Yiyo's (smoked clam, shrimp tacos)
- Mariscos El Zarape (seafood cocktails, clams, ceviche tostados)
- Sabina Restaurante (ceviche, octopus tacos)

Enjoy Parque de la Bandera

Parque Le Bandera, or the Park of the Flag, is a waterfront prome-
nade situated in the downtown area. The open-air park often holds
live music shows. But the best part of Parque Le Bandara is the mu-
sical fountain show that takes place every night at 8 PM.

Hike El Salto Canyon

El Salto is a wonderful place located just 20 miles from the city
center. The beautiful hidden canyon has a 4.9-mile hiking loop with
breathtaking views, stunning water pools, amazing black rock formations and a waterfall. The hike takes only a few hours, but if you have
the time, we recommend spending a night at the campsite.

The hike is full of steep walks, dark crevices, and snaking trails. That's
why it is better to employ a guide if you are unfamiliar with the path.

Surf, ATV, Kayak and Snorkel

Ensenada is an oasis for adventure lovers and one of the best places
to visit for extreme watersports. Surfing is the most popular sport in
this part of Baja and beaches get crowded with surfers on weekends
and in summer. So, if you want less crowd, then fall is the best time
to visit Ensenada for surfing.

In addition to surfing, there are other water sports like snorkeling,
kayaking, fishing trips and much more. You can also hire ATVs to
cruise around the sandy beaches or skydive to look at them from
a new perspective.

Visit the Museums

The Ensenada Museum of History is a perfect place to learn about
how the region developed throughout time. It also portrays the Euro-
pean influence on the growth and development of the city. The museum is located in Riviera del Pacifico Cultural Center, which used to
be a lavish casino in the 20th century.

The second museum to visit is the Regional History Museum. Its building is considered one of the oldest in Ensenada and it contains fossils, bones, artifacts, and ancient information about the landscape, history and culture of Baja California.

Go Sportfishing

Sportfishing in Ensenada is a go-to activity for any fishing enthusiast. It doesn't matter which season you choose as the waters off the coast almost always provide something fun to catch year-round.

Many private owners offer full-day, half-day, and multi-day sportfishing tours that depart from Ensenada Bay. The Pacific Ocean is home to many excellent fish species like rockfish, seabass, calico bass and corvina. If you are fishing in spring and fall, you can hook some Mahi Mahi, several tuna species, and even Yellowtail Amberjack.

Campgrounds in Ensenada

The city of Ensenada does not offer much by way of camping inside the city limits. Most of the camping can be found just north or south of the city, but easily within range of spending quality time exploring all that Ensenada has to offer.

Playa San Miguel

Website:	https://www.facebook.com/SanMiguelVSM/
Phone Number:	+52 646 174 7948
GPS Coordinates:	31.9012, -116.7299
Price Range:	$15 USD

Playa San Miguel is a basic, affordable campground only 10 miles (16 km) north of Ensenada. The campground is incredibly scenic and provides direct access to the rocky beach.

Besides that, the campsite is average and more like a giant parking lot. They provide almost no amenities other than a couple of bathrooms.

Ramona Beach RV Park

Address:	Carretera Tijuana-Ensenada KM 104 Ensenada, BC, Mexico
Website:	Ramona Beach RV Park	Facebook
Phone Number:	+52 646 121 0071
GPS Coordinates:	31.8838, -116.6837
Price Range:	$30 USD

Ramona Beach RV Park is one of the best places to camp near Ensenada. Right on the coast overlooking the ocean, it provides all the essentials to live peacefully and still be within 7 miles (12 km) from the city center.

The beach park has all the hookups with a warm shower and fast internet. Moreover, prices are also quite substantial.

La Jolla Beach Camp

Address:	Carr Rodolfo Sánchez Taboada La Bufadora Banda, B.C Punta Banda o, km 12.5, Ejido Cnel. Esteban Cantú, 22794 Ensenada, B.C., Mexico
Phone Number:	+52 646 154 2005
GPS Coordinates:	31.71742, -116.6648
Price Range:	$20 USD

La Jolla Beach Camp is located at the southern end of Ensenada, pretty close to La Bufadora. It has an excellent location with beautiful and picturesque views. The ground staff is quite friendly, and the campground has all the necessary hookups.

San Quintin

San Quintin is becoming a destination popular with tourists and expats due to its beautiful beaches and wildlife variety. Situated just 185 miles (300 km) south of the US/Mexico border along Highway 1, San Quintin is accessible from the US within a few short hours.

As a collection of 6 small towns, San Quintin is a small city with a population of around 30,000 collectively. The area was first populated by a small group of British colonists that planted wheat, developed a gristmill and were constructing a railway to link with the tracks in California when a drought hit.

The devastating drought destroyed the first harvest and all British colonists left San Quintin by 1900. The gristmill, pier, railway causeway, and an English cemetery are still present along the inner bay.

San Quintin is the agricultural center of the Baja peninsula and the world's largest producer of tomatoes. Along the highway, the ocean side is dominated by vast fields of tomatoes, with other local crops dominating the western side. Strawberries, chili pepper, cucumbers and green beans are the star of the agricultural center.

In addition to agriculture, San Quintin is also working on aquaculture, running conservation projects to repopulate abalone. Moreover, several companies are investing in developing shellfish (oysters and mussels) to harvest and export.

Not only does San Quintin offer its own list of reasons to stop for a few days. But also it is a great place to rest if you are breaking up a long drive to/from the border. You will find many gas stations, hardware shops, supermarkets, banks and other businesses such as propane and water purification stops that cater to travelers.

Things to Do in San Quintin

San Quintin is a perfect combination of beaches, deserts, wetlands, agricultural lands and even an ancient volcanic field. It has some of the most extraordinary places filled with rich history, wildlife and beautiful landscapes.

And it also provides visitors with many sportfishing, clamming, scuba diving, snorkeling and beach exploration options.

Here are some of the top things to do in San Quintin.

Visit La Lobera

La Lobera is a natural crater located on the southern seashore just 25 miles (40 km) away from San Quintin. La Lobera is simply enormous, with a depth of more than 50 feet. The magnificent cave is home to seals and sea lions, where you can meditate with the sounds of crashing waves on the rocky walls.

In order to reach La Lobera, you have to drive through the desert. So, it's best to access via an ATV or 4x4 vehicle.

Explore the Wetlands

The wetlands of San Quintin Bay are of great importance in the peninsula. San Quintin is a sanctuary for more than 400 species of local and migratory birds and is considered the lungs of Baja. The lands are spread across a large area where you can enjoy kayaking and birdwatching.

When visiting the wetlands, always respect the environment. It is a delicate area that deserves caution when driving, hiking and otherwise exploring.

Attend the Tomato and Wine Festival

The tomato and Wine festival is celebrated annually in August to promote the local tomato culture. San Quintin is the largest exporter of tomatoes and plays a vital role in Mexico's economy.

You can taste many local tomato-based dishes with fine wines from Mexico at the festival. Moreover, there are many fun contests and live performances from local bands.

Enjoy Water Activities

San Quintin has a vast shoreline. The beautiful coast has all the facilities to enjoy aquatic activities, including surfing, snorkeling, scuba diving, sport fishing and boating.

San Quintin coast is home to many marine animals, which makes it an ideal place for observing marine life through your favorite activities - whether boating, kayaking or paddleboarding.

Cabo San Quintin and Punta Arrecife are the go-to places for snorkeling and diving. The beaches have crystal clear water, beautiful rock formations, colorful flora and algae beds where millions of colorful fish feed and shelter. Moreover, you can also find some lobsters and scallops in deeper water.

Explore the Beaches

San Quintin has one of the finest shorelines in the Baja California region. The crystal-clear water, white sand beaches, excellent water activities and abundance of beautiful aquatic animals add to the charm of the beaches.

Go Bird Watching

Bird watching is a must-do activity whenever you visit San Quintin. As mentioned above, the area has exceptional avian wildlife. It is home to more than 400 bird species and sightings of millions of migratory birds along the shoreline, in the wetlands and city are common year-round.

Try Clamming

Along with tomatoes, San Quintin is known for its seemingly endless supply of Pismo clams and mussels. Pismo clams can grow up to six inches, and the fertile volcanic soil, rich minerals, and nutrients brought by the ocean current produce a perfect habitat for clams and oysters. Digging for oysters and clams in shallow water is a popular activity in the area.

You can easily find clams and oysters along the shoreline, especially on Santa Maria Beach.

Campgrounds in San Quintin

Most of the campgrounds in the San Quintin area are scattered throughout the region. But all will leave you close enough to enjoy your favorite activities while staying here.

Adele's Ranch Camping

Website:	Baja California Adele's RANCH Converted bus, Camping and Casita rental	Facebook
Phone Number:	+52 616 104 7858
GPS Coordinates:	30.76946, -116.0421
Price Range:	$10 USD

Adele's Ranch is a scenic postcard-like campground surrounded by strawberry farms with a beautiful beach to add to its allure. If you are not a fussy traveler open to dry camping, this campground will be sufficient for you to be able to enjoy the area.

Cielito Lindo RV Park

Address:	Lote A y B Manzana 21 San Quintin, BC, Mexico
Website:	Hotel Restaurant and Bar Cielito Lindo	Facebook
Phone Number:	+52 616 103 3169
GPS Coordinates:	30.4093, -115.9242
Price Range:	$7 - 10 USD

Cielito Lindo is a decent RV park not far from Santa Maria beach. The campground has free and fast WiFi, hot showers, and electric, water and sewer hookups. The RV park also has an excellent restaurant and bar known for its crab claws and delicious margaritas, which you can enjoy during daily happy hour throughout the week.

Fidel's Palapas RV Park

Phone Number: +52 616 105 3957

GPS Coordinates: 30.3790, -115.8687

Price Range: $12 USD

Like other camping options, Fidel's El Pabellon also comes with stunning views of the Pacific Ocean. The beachside RV park has electricity and a water hookup.

Moreover, the owner is very friendly and the park has good Wi-Fi and hot showers, though the bathroom could be better. You can even ask for a home-cooked lobster dinner here!

Catavina

Catavina, the rock garden of Baja, is a small town located midway through Baja California Norte and approximately 75 miles (120 km) south of El Rosario. The landscape changes drastically when you enter Catavina. Volcanic boulders stack on top of each other with enormous cacti to create a surreal visual experience as though you were on another planet.

Catavina is more of a rest area for travelers and truck drivers than it is a multi-day destination. It is around 7 to 8 hours away from US/Mexico border, which makes it an excellent stop if you're scrambling north or south.

The town has only 150-200 residents and you will not find many restaurants and hotels. There are a couple of restaurants, rustic motels, one RV park and a proper hotel called Hotel Mision with dining and a pool.

One thing to note before planning a trip to Catavina is the scarcity of fuel in this stretch of Highway 1. You won't find any formal gas stations nearby and locals will sell gas out of drums as the nearest gas stations are either 2 hours to the north in El Rosario or to the south in Villa Jesus Maria.

The gas is expensive, and the quality is questionable. But if you don't plan accordingly, you have to bear that because it's the only option.

Things to Do in Catavina

There is not much to do in Catavina outside of exploring the desert landscape filled with unique rocks and cactus. You can enjoy ATV rides along the enormous boulders or can camp under the beautiful milky way.

Here are the top things to do in Catavina.

Walk Among the Giant Cardon

Catavina is a very fertile area for cacti. There are over 80 types of cacti growing in the region, including agave, nopal, pitahaya, yucca, and cholla. But the unique one is Giant Caradon or Elephant Cactus.

The Cardon is native to the Baja California peninsula, can grow up to 60 feet and weighs up to 10 tons. Moreover, they can live for more than 200 years.

Explore the Catavina Boulder Field

The Catavina Boulder Fields, or the rock garden, is fantastic and strange at the same time. It is one of the most popular tourist attractions in the area. The field has thousands of building-sized boulders and granite rocks coexisting with beautiful flora and lovely natural freshwater pools

The stunning landscape is a must-visit whenever you are traveling through Baja.

Visit The Colonial Missions

There are ruins of two colonial missions in Catavina. The San Fernando Velicata and Santa Maria de Los Angles Missions were built in the late 18th Century to convert Cochimi Indians. But they were abandoned in 1818 after failing.

The San Fernando de Velicata mission is accessible without 4WD but does require a guide. While the Santa Maria de Los Angeles Mission is located approximately 15 miles down a road with extreme 4-wheel drive conditions.

Cave Paintings

Cave paintings are located just a half mile north of Catavina. The paintings and pictographs are estimated to be up to 10,000 years old and are believed to be drawn by Cochimi Indians.

No one exactly knows what the paintings are. Several theories go from witchery and religious purposes to important events. They are relatively easily accessible just off the highway.

Go On An ATV/Dirt Bike

The rugged town has the perfect terrain for ATVs and dirt bike rides. If you're traveling with ATVs or other 4x4 vehicles you can get off-road and feel as though you are on an adventure on another planet!

Remember to always carry a portable GPS to easily follow the trail because getting lost in the Catavina desert is relatively easy.

Campgrounds in Catavina

Rancho Santa Yenz

Address:	22969 Santa Ynés, Baja California, Mexico
GPS Coordinates:	29.7295, -114.6963
Price Range:	$10 USD

Rancho Santa Yenz is your only option for formal camping in or around Catavina. It is a rustic campground located 1 mile off Highway 1. With around 40 campsites, there is almost always room available and at modest prices.

But keep in mind you will be dry camping. It does not have any hookups. You will get water in buckets and the bathroom is a part of the owner's house.

Destinations Along Highway 5

Federal Highway 5 stretches from the border city of Mexicali all the way south to where it unites with Highway 1 after 250 miles (400 km) of mostly well-maintained road. San Felipe is the largest town along this route. But there are several great destinations along the way well worth your attention.

San Felipe

San Felipe is among the most popular tourist destinations in Baja. It is on the northwestern shore of the Sea of Cortez, located just 125 miles (200 km) south of the US/Mexico border along a very well-maintained Highway 5.

The city is one of the fastest-growing resort towns on the peninsula. Despite being a fast-growing town, the former fishing village has retained most of its original charm.

Like most coastal cities in Baja, San Felipe has a warm, dry winter climate and hot and humid summer. It is one of the primary getaways for first-time and every-time campers wanting to escape the colder northern US and Canadian winters.

For this reason there is a lot of tourist infrastructure and many times you will find that prices are posted in US Dollars rather than Mexican pesos because of the tourist presence that dominates the city.

Most tourists and retirees arrive during the "snowbird season" (November through March). With increasing tourism, San Felipe is starting to grow significantly. Many US-style condos, communities, high-end resorts, housings, marinas and golf courses are developing.

Moreover, massive investment from retirees seeking affordable real estate can be seen throughout the shoreline.

San Felipe has a lot to offer for visitors of every age. A walk along the

Malecon will provide you opportunity to dine at some of the best seafood restaurants and street food stalls in Baja. And there are plenty of beaches there for a peaceful walk, jog, or swim.

You can embark on fishing trips to witness the traditional Mexican way of fishing. Or you can go off-road on ATVs in the vast open desert.

San Felipe really comes alive, for better or for worse, both during the Baja off-road races (during fall) and the Semana Santa holy week (typically early April).

Things to Do in San Felipe

San Felipe offers a variety of attractions, from top-notch restaurants and excellent fish tacos to exceptional beaches, sport fishing and off-roading in the desert. The town has something for everyone.

Here are the best things to do in San Felipe.

Enjoy the Malecon

The Malecon is the town's boardwalk located in the center of San Felipe. It is the seawall passing along the main beach area that is lined with restaurants, stores and street vendors of all sorts. The Malecon is quite lively throughout the day, especially at night.

There are numerous street food vendors selling fish and shrimp tacos, traditional Mexican cuisine, and much more.

You will also find various fish charter boat services where you can book your sport fishing tour.

Get Offroad in the Desert

Offroad desert adventures are a popular activity in San Felipe. The city is surrounded by a vast open desert where you can get dirty on dune buggies, ATVs, and dirt bikes.

Offroad vehicles are readily available for rent in San Felipe and you'll hear the sound of them racing around town at all hours of the day and night.

Spend a Day at Beach

If all you want to do is spend time at the beach, San Felipe is a great first destination to wet your toes in the Sea of Cortez. Most campgrounds offer camping at or near the beach so you can walk out of your RV and be on the sand in minutes.

The seaside town has a handful of different beaches where you can relax, swim, kayak or paddleboard to your heart's content.

Savor the Fresh Seafood

You can enjoy fresh seafood all over San Felipe. Founded as a fishing village, the city has tons of options, especially in the central area along the Malecon. If you're craving a tasty fish or shrimp taco there are plenty of places to dine.

In addition to seafood, many restaurants and street food vendors also offer traditional Mexican food like carne asada and tacos al pastor (a personal favorite of ours!).

Some popular seafood places in San Felipe are:

- La Vaquita
- Mariscos La Morena
- Resturante El Popular Kiko
- Taco Factory
- Chuy's Place

Embark on Sportfishing Trip

Sportfishing is arguably the most popular attraction in San Felipe as the town has everything to provide an exceptional experience. From excellent weather, great fishing crews and a variety of fish that you can catch throughout the year, you can't go wrong chartering a trip or taking your own boat out of San Felipe.

Moreover, the city lies on the coast of the prolific Sea of Cortez, habitat for some of the best fish including sailfish, marlin, amberjack, pacific sierra, snook and, triggerfish.

Many one-day sportfishing expeditions are available in San Felipe. For fishing fanatics, San Felipe also has a couple of big boats that can go on multi-day fishing tours.

Soak in the Hot Springs at Puertecitos

Puertecitos is a small settlement around a beautiful cove located around 45 minutes south of San Felipe. It has a few natural hot springs, where you can enjoy the incredible natural sauna. You will also find a campsite near the hot springs.

The best way to enjoy the hot springs and cove is to visit throughout the day. Before arriving, check the tide so that you arrive at the right time when the tide is slowly going down.

Stroll through the Valley of Giants

El Valle de Los Gigantes, or the Valley of the Giants, is a natural reserve of enormous Cardon cacti. Located just 30 minutes south of San Felipe, the Punta Estrella Ranch is the access point for the Valley of the Giants.

The desert forest has hundreds of Cardon cacti, many over 100 years old and 60 feet high. The destination is quite popular among photographers, especially during sunsets.

It cost around $10 USD to spend the day among the giants and a portion of the reserve is drivable without 4WD. However, if you have a 4WD vehicle you can go further into the desert landscape or you can park and walk around.

Volunteer in San Felipe

Horses In Baja

("Centro Ecuestre Caballerizas Paraiso") If you're looking for a unique opportunity to both volunteer and/or camp and you love horses and children, then you'll want to consider giving Lynn a call or email to connect with the Centro Ecuestre Caballerizas Paraiso organization just north of the town of San Felipe.

Lynn brings children with a range of physical and mental disabilities to her ranch and uses equine-assisted therapy to help the children develop. Whether you find yourself mucking stalls and feeding horses or walking with the children as they ride on the back of the horses, this is a truly unique opportunity to volunteer in San Felipe.

Plus Lynn offers camping by donation and trail rides if you want to go horseback riding. Although you are several miles inland, the desert sunrises and sunsets are spectacular and worth a visit on their own.

Check out the Facebook Page for contact information or email Lynn directly.

Campgrounds in San Felipe

Pete's Camp RV Park

Address:	Hwy 5 KM-178 San Felipe, BC, Mexico
Website:	www.petescamp.com
Phone Number:	+52 951 694 6704
GPS Coordinates:	31.1348, -114.8888
Price Range:	$55 USD

Pete's Camp is a large RV resort on the north end of San Felipe. As it caters to the ex-pat crowd, there are ample big-rig-friendly full hook-up RV sites and a restaurant/bar on site. Each of the 37 campsites is on the beach on a level concrete pad with full hookups.

There are both pull-through and pull up sites catering to all types of RVs. Overall, the bathrooms are clean and all hookups work perfectly. But expect to pay a hefty price, especially if you have a tow vehicle as there is an additional nightly fee for non-RV vehicles.

Note: You are now required to make reservations at least 2 weeks in advance if you want to stay at Pete's Camp. And it is advisable that you book well in advance, particularly during the busy winter season.

Campo Turistico 1

Address:	Av. Mar de Cortes Sur 888, Centro, 21850 San Felípe, B.C., Mexico
Website:	https://www.facebook.com/campo1oficial/
Phone Number:	+52 686 193 1712
GPS Coordinates:	31.0392, -114.8250
Price Range:	$25 USD

(Electric is 20 amp only)

Campo Touristico 1 is located on the north side of San Felipe just far enough away from the city center to offer more solitude and quiet than other options but still close enough that you can enjoy everything San Felipe has to offer.

It is run by a friendly Mexican family that goes out of their way to make you feel at home. With private beach access at the base of a mountain, you can enjoy the incredible landscape with options to both dry camp or have 20 amp electrical service.

There is a dump station on site as well as showers and a restroom to accommodate the 30 sites.

La Palapa RV Camp

Address:	Golfo de California #92, Segunda Secc, San Felipe, 21850 San Felípe, B.C., Mexico
Website:	https://www.facebook.com/Lapalaparvcamp/
GPS Coordinates:	31.0336, -114.8281
Price Range:	$25 USD

La Palapa RV Camp is located on the north side of the Malecon in the heart of San Felipe. The small campground has an excellent layout where you can have your very own palapa (hut) on the beach. And the staff is quite nice and friendly.

The campsite also has 24 hours security and CCTV cameras. Moreover, the bathrooms are also well-maintained and clean. And due to it's central location, it is just a short walk to the Malecon.

Kiki's RV Camping & Hotel

Address:	Av, Golfo de California No.80, 21850 San Felípe, B.C., Mexico
Website:	http://www.kiki.com.mx/
Phone Number:	+52 686 577 2021
GPS Coordinates:	31.0345, -114.8279
Price Range:	$25 USD

Kiki's RV Camping & Hotel is located in town just a few minutes walk to the Malecon. With 25 sites that can accommodate RVs of all sizes, you'll find all the amenities you could want in a campground for a reasonable rate.

Sites offer full hookups with 20 and 30 amp electrical connections, Wi-Fi and a restroom. You can have your own palapa and end up with a beach view if you make reservations in advance.

Seaside Hotel & Victor's RV Park

Address:	Av. Mar de Cortes Sur, Mar de Cortés, 21850 San Felípe, B.C., Mexico
Website:	Seaside Hotel & Victors RV Park San Felipe B.C. | Facebook
Phone Number:	+52 686 577 2817
GPS Coordinates:	31.0134, -114.8352
Price Range:	$30 USD

On the south side of town, just a ten minute walk from the Malecon, Victor's RV Park offers beachside and inland camping options for RVs of all sorts. Although it is a slightly expensive option, the campground offers both dry camping and full hookup options, an on-site restaurant and friendly staff.

You can easily fit big rigs and the campground has excellent Wi-Fi availability. Our favorite part of staying at Victor's RV Park is catching up with Lilly, the owner, who is incredibly friendly and remembers us year after year.

Best Boondocking /Alternative Camping Option

Horses In Baja ("Centro Ecuestre Caballerizas Paraiso"). Although not technically boondocking, as Lynn offers her property for camping by donation, this is the most affordable, reliable and safe dry camping option in San Felipe.

Camp in the desert landscape of the El Dorado development where sunrises and sunsets are incredible, you can go on horseback rides and can even volunteer to assist Lynn with her children's equine-assisted therapy sessions.

Check out the Facebook Page for contact information or email Lynn directly.

Puertecitos

Puertecitos is a small town located around 50 miles (90 km) south of San Felipe along Federal Highway 5. It is a small town of roughly 200-300 homes, many of which are vacation homes of retirees and expatriates from the US and Canada.

The town, permanently settled in 1949, is a part of the San Felipe municipality, so the climate is pretty much the same.

Puertecitos is primarily known for its natural hot springs built into the rocky coastline. The town has a couple of new hotels, restaurants, and campsites.

Some vacation homes and trailers are also available on Airbnb. Moreover, fuel is not readily available.

Things to Do in Puertecitos

Puertecitos is a small settlement mainly known for its beautiful cove, hot springs and a couple of beaches. It is a lovely town, but you will not find much else.

Here are the things you can do in Puertecitos.

Soak in the Hot Springs

The rocky sulfurous water pools on the coastline of Puertecitos are an ideal place to immerse and relax. The hot springs are built into the rocks that line the seashore and are surrounded by the beauty of the Baja California region. There are several different springs with varying temperatures so you have options when you visit.

The water can be quite hot at low tide, so it's better to choose the time when the tide is higher. In this way, the cool salty Sea of Cortez overflows into the pools, making the temperature perfect to soak in and enjoy stunning views of beautiful coastlines, dolphins and pelicans.

Moreover, there is a campsite nearby where you can stay for the day to enjoy the views thoroughly. Camping is around $30 USD per night, which includes access to the hot springs.

If you are just looking to visit the hot springs for the day, it cost around $25 USD. So if you are able, it's worth planning to spend the extra $5 to camp so you can enjoy the hot springs at night beneath the stars!

Enjoy the Beaches

Along the shoreline, you will find a mixture of beautiful rocky and sandy beaches. Puertecitos has a gorgeous landscape, and some of the beaches are simply stunning.

Head out on a SUP/Kayak

In addition, to stunning beaches, you will also find many kayaking and paddle boarding opportunities in the town. Kayakers can enjoy the true desert and sea wilderness in some parts of Puertecitos.

As mentioned above, it is a small area, but its sea and geography are pretty diverse. You could find finback whales, grey whales, dolphins, sea lions, sea birds and sea turtles in the nearby water along with small islands and hidden coves.

Campgrounds in Puertecitos

Puertecitos RV Park

Address:	A Puertecitos, Playas de San Felipe, 22964 San Felípe, B.C., Mexico
GPS Coordinates:	30.3501, -114.6401
Price Range:	$30 USD

Puertecitos is an affordable beachfront campground near the hot springs. The campsite has most of the amenities needed for a comfortable stay. The electricity is good, the water and toilets are clean, and each site has a grill, picnic table and shade to relax and enjoy on the beach.

Bahia San Luis Gonzaga (Gonzaga Bay)

Bahia San Luis Gonzaga is another treasure of Baja. The peaceful bay is a must-visit if you are driving through Baja along Highway 5. Gonzaga Bay is located around 3 hours South of San Felipe (100 miles, 160 km) and holds the beauty of some of the stunning sandy beaches, warm and crystal-clear water, incredible ocean wildlife and coves.

Reaching Gonzaga Bay after turning off the highway involves traversing some mostly hard-packed dirt roads, with several destinations requiring 4WD. But the bumpy washboards are worth the beauty and solitude at the end of the road.

Gonzaga Bay has one decent hotel, Alfonsinas, that serves one of the best meals in the area and also organizes fishing and diving trips in the Sea of Cortez. There is a small market that has everything you expect from a regular convenience store which is quite surprising considering the surroundings.

And there is a Pemex gas station that is closed more often than it is open (in other words, don't count on getting fuel here!) Sometimes if it's closed you can get gas from Rancho Grande.

Moreover, there are a few campgrounds with basic amenities, restaurants and an ever-expanding swath of vacation homes of expatriates. You can go on off-road ATV and dirt bike trips or visit the surrounding islands by kayak or SUP across the beautiful Gonzaga Bay.

Moreover, snorkeling is also possible on the sandy beaches of the bay. It has very clean water, and you will see conch, oysters, clams, starfish, goldfish, manta rays and many small species along the coast.

Things to Do in Bahia San Luis Gonzaga

Bahia San Luis Gonzaga is a fairly small town and is still under construction in many areas, but it has much to offer for adventure lovers.

Here are the best things to do in Bahia San Luis Gonzaga.

Enjoy the Beaches

Beautiful white sand beaches are a trademark of Baja. Bahia San Luis Gonzaga has some of the most incredible beaches, still a bit off the beaten path so not as spoiled as others in the peninsula. They are a perfect place to relax and meditate on the sound of gently lapping waves.

Moreover, the nights are even more stunning here as there is no proper development for hundreds of miles in any direction. Enjoy peaceful surroundings, beautiful starry skies and the sounds of waves washing ashore.

Go Kayaking or Paddleboarding

Kayaking and standup paddle boarding are excellent activities to do in Gonzaga Bay. You can kayak to nearby islands and other beaches in the area. Moreover, small kayak fishing tours are also possible.

You can use any of the beaches if you have your own kayak or paddleboard. Otherwise, you can rent kayaks from Rancho Grande.

Try Snorkeling

Bahia San Luis Gonzaga is an ideal place for snorkeling. The beaches have crystal clear water, with a wide variety of fish species. Even at the beach, you will see starfish, shellfish, oysters and manta rays.

You can book snorkeling and boating trips at Alfonsina and Rancho Grande. The boat rides can also take you to the Enchanted Islands and beaches of Punta Final, a harder to reach destination at the southern end of the bay. Punta Final has some lovely coves and beautiful beaches, making it ideal for snorkeling and kayaking.

Go Fishing

Fishing is another great thing to do in Gonzaga Bay. The bay is more isolated and has not been as overfished as other areas of Baja. Thus there are tons of fish species and catching them is not difficult. Yellowtail, sea bass, triggerfish, corvina, pompano and a variety of grouper are commonly caught in San Luis Gonzaga.

The sea of Cortez is also a playing field for dolphins and a variety of whales. While fishing, you might spot some whale sharks if you are lucky.

If you aren't traveling with your own fishing boat or kayak, you can book fishing tours at Alfonsina Hotel and Rancho Grande campground.

Campgrounds in Bahia San Luis Gonzaga

Campgrounds in Bahia San Luis Gonzaga are mostly informal dry camping destinations where you're basically paying for the view. These are the two most common places to camp along Gonzaga Bay.

Rancho Grande

Website:	https://www.facebook.com/Rancho-Grande-170553939718804/
Phone Number:	+52 646 386 0817
GPS Coordinates:	29.789, -114.3951
Price Range:	$15 USD

Rancho Grande is located right beside the Alfonsina Hotel. The massive campground has beachfront camping areas with a palapa and grill.

The palapas at the beach are more like a hut where you can put chairs or bind hammocks and enjoy the beautiful Sea of Cortez.

Campo Beluga

Phone Number:	+52 664 416 9965
GPS Coordinates:	29.7750, -114.3844
Price Range:	$25 USD

Campo Beluga is a great place to spend a few nights along Gonzaga Bay. The camp is slightly expensive for what it has to offer. But it does have limited running water to be able to grab a bucket shower if needed and decent toilets and showers (cold).

If you are traveling with friends, or make friends on the way there, you can often split the camping fee since they charge per palapa and each palapa can fit 2 or more campers.

Bahia de Los Angeles

Far from everything, Bahia de Los Angeles is not an average bustling Mexican town. Rather, it is a small village tucked away down a gorgeous 60-mile (95 km) stretch of highway with rugged mountains, a vast desert, huge cacti and the stunning blue Sea of Cortez hemming it in.

The town is, without a doubt, one of the treasures of Baja California if not only for its remote location. It is one of the finest places to visit for adventure and sea lovers who want to experience the extraordinary beauty of nature while being mostly off-grid.

Don't expect cell service or even WiFi at local businesses in town that offer it. In Bahia de Los Angeles you are about as off-grid as you can be while still having access to grocery stores, restaurants, small shops and fuel.

As an offshoot of Federal Highway 1, the road into Bahia de Los Angeles is paved, easy to drive and the long journey is rewarded by the incredible landscape. The breathtaking and scenic ride through the desert mountains with "Dr. Seuss-like" cacti set the tone for the upcoming adventures in Bahia de Los Angeles.

Bahia de Los Angeles was established as a fishing village now with around 1,000 residents, most of which are fishermen and former miners. It used to be one of the remote areas of Baja, but because of its position and popularity among tourists, the area is developing quickly.

All throughout Baja you'll hear tourist-speak call it "Bay of LA" or "BOLA" as it has risen in popularity recently. Moreover, much development is underway to enhance accommodation options, internet access, waste disposal, and other necessary amenities.

The weather of Bahia de Los Angeles is usually warm due to the desert, though the wind can pick up with little notice and offer some of the best wind sports opportunities on the peninsula. Whale sharks will also migrate as far north in the Sea of Cortez as Bahia de Los Angeles, but only when the water is warmest, typically between July and November.

The Mexican government is actively working on conserving marine life in Bahia de Los Angeles. The surrounding 16 islands and several small islands around the bay are the nesting grounds for five sea turtle species and reserves for endangered species. Moreover, there's also a private sea turtle research center. Tourists can also visit the research center to see the beautiful creatures up close.

There are several places to camp in the Bahia de Los Angeles. You can virtually camp anywhere in the bay at Playa La Gringa. However, there are a couple of excellent campgrounds that offer good amenities, such as Daggett's and Campo Archelon.

Watersports, aqua tourism and fishing are the primary source of income for the locals. You will find all sorts of watersport activities and fishing trips in the bay. Moreover, a couple of museums cover local mining history and a collection of fish skeletons.

Things to Do in Bahia de Los Angeles

Bahia de Los Angeles is a place with a wondrous landscape and fabulous marine life with a perfect climate to provide an unforgettable experience.

Here are the top things to do in Bahia de Los Angeles.

Enjoy All the Watersports

The Bay of Los Angeles is an excellent spot for watersports. Places like Villa Bahia Hotel and Daggett's Campground offer free kayaks when you stay there. In addition to exploring the water just off the coast, the nearby islands provide some excellent opportunities to enjoy watersports. The crystal-clear water with diverse marine life creates an ideal snorkeling and scuba diving environment.

Moreover, paddleboarding and kayaking around 16 surrounding islands in the Sea of Cortez is a magnificent experience. While paddling, you might see dolphins, sea lions, marine birds, whale sharks and fin whales.

Head Out Sportsfishing

Once overfishing considerably reduced the fish in the bay. But the conservation efforts from the Mexican government have really increased the number and species of fish in the water. Now Bahia de Los Angeles is a world-famous place for sport fishing.

The bay is mainly known for yellowtail but also has bass, cabrilla, barracuda, skipjack, grouper and roosterfish. In summer, you might even catch a marlin or sailfish.

If you aren't traveling with your own boat, you can hire local fishermen to take you to the best spots as the main fishing area is around the neighboring islands.

Swim with Whale Sharks

Bahia de Los Angeles has a great variety of life under the water and is a playground for dolphins, whale sharks, and grey whales. It is possible to swim next to whale sharks between June and November (when the water is warmest).

You can book boats from hotels and campgrounds to dive with the gentle giants of the ocean. Moreover, you will also see dolphins, sea lions and sea turtles.

Go Whale Watching

In addition to the dolphins, sea lions and whale sharks that are abundant in Bahia de Los Angeles, both grey whales and fin whales will migrate through the area seasonally. Both whales are most likely to be present November through April as they follow the warmer waters and abundance of food.

You can book tours to head out and watch the magnificent creatures as they prepare for their long summer migrations.

Visit the Nature and Culture Museum

The nature and culture museum is the main cultural attraction of Bahia de Los Angeles. It is located in the downtown area behind Bahia de Los Angeles delegation. The museum has a mixture of bones from mammoths, dolphins, whales and dinosaurs.

Moreover, you will also see some mining artifacts of the 19th century along with illustrations and historical pictures. The visiting hours vary but are typically 9 am to 12 pm and 2 pm to 4 pm and the museum remains closed during August and September.

Explore the Mision San Francisco Borja de Adac

The Mision de San Francisco Borja is an 18th-century mission in a region known to the Cochimi people. Construction took place over 42 years between 1759 and 1801 and ended up being abandoned less than 20 years later. It was rebuilt as a quarry by the Dominican order and was abandoned and looted several times.

Now it is open to the public to as one of the dozens of missions scattered throughout Baja that tell the story of this chapter in history through the remaining architecture of the buildings.

Day Trip to La Isla Coronado

Isla Corondo lies just off the eastern end of Bahia de Los Angeles. It is a 7-kilometer island with a beautiful landscape accompanied by beautiful lagoons, incredible marine life, and a wide variety of reptiles on land. The island is also surrounded by excellent snorkeling and scuba diving spots.

If you do not have your own boat, you can hire a guide from hotels and campgrounds in Bahia de Los Angeles.

See the Cave Paintings of Montevideo

A little off the beaten path, though still accessible, the cave paintings of Montevideo are considered some of the oldest and most important in the Baja peninsula. They are a great abstract presentation of animal figures and geometric designs that date up to 10,000 years ago.

The paintings are located 14 miles (22 km) from Bahia de Los Angeles on the road leading to the Mission of San Borja following the Montevideo stream. It is advisable that you travel by 4WD vehicles to reach both the cave paintings and the mission.

Campgrounds in Bahia de Los Angeles

Although there is ample room to camp along Playa La Gringa, there are two popular campgrounds in Bahia de Los Angeles that attract the most travelers.

Campo Archelon

Address:	Campo Archelon 22830 Ensenada, México CAMPO ARCHELON, 22830 Bahía de los Ángeles, B.C., Mexico
Phone Number:	+52 646 273 9936
GPS Coordinates:	28.9720, -113.5469
Price Range:	$10 USD

Campo Archelon is a beautiful beachfront campground with palapas and picnic tables. Once a sea turtle research center, it has since been converted into the most popular campground in Bahia de Los Angeles. Archelon also has an urban style restaurant offering craft beers, food, and coffee.

There are hot showers, clean toilets, and water. The Wi-Fi is as good as it gets in Bahia de Los Angeles. And you can expect to see quite a few species of birds during your stay.

Daggett's Beach Camping

GPS Coordinates: 28.9795, -113.5468

Price Range: $20 USD

Daggett's Beach Camping is another beautiful beachfront campground. However, it does not have a lot of amenities. There is no electricity, Wi-Fi is very slow, showers are cold with less water pressure and sites don't have water and sewer hookups.

But this is a popular place to stay if you plan to spend some time fishing and you can camp right on the beach.

Best Boondocking /Alternative Camping Option

Playa La Gringa. By far the best and most popular place to boondock in Bahia de Los Angeles is Playa La Gringa. Located a few miles to the north of town along a sometimes rugged dirt road, Playa La Gringa offers a long stretch of rocky and pebbly beach on which to camp.

If you want to really feel like you are away from things, boondocking here will give you a true escape even from the remote town of Bahia de Los Angeles. Although the beach had a bad security rep for a few years, it is safe to camp and, like anytime boondocking, just be aware of your surroundings and consider camping with friends.

CHAPTER 4

Where to Go in Baja California Sur

We have divided this chapter about places to visit in the southern state of Baja California into 2 sections based on the geography of the peninsula.

The first section will address destinations from the border of Baja California to the capital city of La Paz. This will cover locations along the singular Highway 1 as it criss-crosses from the Pacific Ocean to the Sea of Cortez.

The second section will address destinations on the southern tip of the peninsula encompassing both the "East Cape," or southeastern edge of Baja California Sur, as well as the western edge of the state along the Pacific Ocean. Here, the highway splits into two and makes a loop through this part of the peninsula.

Both sections will cover Baja California Sur from north to south as though you were traveling through the peninsula along Highway 1 after crossing from Baja California.

Destinations to the North

Baja California Sur is a spectacular place to visit. Although the entire state is still dependent upon Federal Highway 1 running its length from top to bottom, there are plenty of great places to stop and spend a few days, weeks or months.

These are the first destinations you'll approach as you cross the border from Baja California.

Guerrero Negro

Guerrero Negro is not at the top of the list for any traveler, except those who know to seek out the grey whales during their annual migration along the Pacific coast. Otherwise, the town has little to be desired and acts more like a rest stop than a destination in itself.

You can meet all sorts of logistical needs in Guerrero Negro - from groceries and purified water to fuel, propane and dump stations located in a handful of campgrounds in town. Virtually everything you need is located along the main road leading to and from town off Highway 1.

Located at the northernmost border with Baja California, Guerrero Negro is not an average Baja California Sur town as the weather is quite different. It seems almost northern California-esque as it stays cloudy most of the time with the average temperature around 67F.

Interestingly, the city is located on the edge of the Vizcaino Desert. Although it does not appear desirable, Guerrero Negro has something special to offer travelers. From January to April, the magnificent grey whales come to give birth in nearby lagoons as it is the first stop they make on their long journey from Alaska.

This in itself is worth the stop, particularly as you will drive through magnificently colored salt flats that produce over seven million tons of salt per year.

Guerrero Negro was founded in 1957 as a salt camp. Initially called Salina Vizcaino, the name was later changed to Guerrero Negro, which means "black warrior," after a ship that sank there in the mid-19th century.

In addition to whales and salt works, there are giant dunes that seem to magnificently melt into the ocean. The scenic place is an excellent spot for photographers.

Things to Do in Guerrero Negro

Although there is not much to do in Guerrero Negro, the things worth coming for really are worth the visit.

Here are the best things to do in Guerrero Negro.

Go Whale Watching in Scammon's Lagoon

Scammon's Lagoon, or Lagoon Ojo de Liebre, is the largest biosphere reserve in Latin America. It was discovered in 1857 by American whaling captain Charles Melville Scammon who used to slaughter whales for whale oil, bones, and meat.

This nearly brought the gentle giants to extinction. But in 1971 the Mexican government took steps and created Grey Whale Sanctuary to ensure the survival of the species.

Scammon's lagoon welcomes the whales in January and they stay until the middle of April. This is the first location of their 6,000-mile journey from the cool summer waters of the Bering and Chukchi sea to warmer winter waters.

The grey whales stay in Scammon's Lagoon in winter, and the protected, warm water of the lagoon creates an ideal environment to give birth to their 1,000-pound calves.

All the tour operators are located on the one main street from where you can easily book your trip. Moreover, you can also book whale watching trips from some hotels. Whale-watching season is incredibly busy, so booking your tours in advance is recommended.

Do note that all boat captains should not chase after the whales. Instead, they take you near to where whales are congregating and the whales will actually approach the boat. If you manage to make eye contact with one of these gentle giants you will have an experience that will change your life!

Drive Through The Salt Flats

Guerrero Negro salt works is the largest evaporative salt production facility in the world. It produces almost six million tons of salt annually, which is exported mainly to the Pacific basin. It is a 65 miles facility and economically sustains the town's entire population.

Driving through the salt flats is otherworldly. As you follow hard-packed dirt roads, you'll be led from one large pond to the next, each one strangely colored in hues of pink. Aside from the roads and occasional signs, you might feel as though you were driving on Mars as you will likely not see another vehicle for miles of driving.

Visit the Dunas de Soledad

The Dunas de Soledad is an enormous area of barren dunes just north of the town of Guerrero Negro. There is no vegetation and the landscape constantly changes because of changing winds offering a new portrait nearly every day. The best time to visit the area is around dusk and dawn to experience the stunning sunrise and sunset over the dunes.

Enjoy Osprey Watching

Ospreys are magnificent birds that elegantly glide through the air and are often found with fish between their talons. The majestic species have a big population in Guerrero Negro.

Due to their nesting habits, large nests have been prepared for them on or near power poles. The mounts of the poles are specially built for ospreys to give them ample space and to entice them away from nesting where they would otherwise be unwelcomed.

You'll find ospreys hunting the waters all around Guerrero Negro.

Visit Malarrimo Restaurant

Malarrimo restaurant has a small museum with a nice collection of washed-out things recovered from Malarrimo Beach. It includes everything from sandblasted bottles and fishing floats from Japan to pieces of ships, oars, army containers, construction helmets, shipping wheels, and much more.

Campgrounds in Guerrero Negro

Mario's RV Park

Address:	Transpeninsular Hwy Km. 217.3 Sin Colonia, 23940 Guerrero Negro, B.C.S., Mexico
Website:	http://mariostours.com/rvpark.html
Phone Number:	+52 615 157 1940
GPS Coordinates:	27.9837, -114.0135
Price Range:	$15 USD

Mario's RV Park is located just north of town and is one of the best options both for camping and for sourcing a whale watching tour as they arrange and lead tours during season. With 40 full-hookup spots large enough to accommodate big rigs, this campground will be about the best you will find in Guerrero Negro.

With an onsite restaurant and reasonably reliable WiFi, you'll also have access to clean restrooms with hot showers.

Malarrimo RV Park

Address:	Emiliano Zapata 75, Loma Bonita, 23940 Guerrero Negro, B.C.S., Mexico
Website:	http://malarrimo.com/
Phone Number:	+52 615-157-0100
GPS Coordinates:	27.9716, -114.0302
Price Range:	$20 - 25 USD

Malirrimo offers over 20 big-rig friendly campsites in mostly level and sort-of paved pads. It is an excellent option if you want to stay closer to the city. It is within walking distance from the city center and all you could want or need to do in Guerrero Negro.

There is 20-amp electricity, satisfactory Wi-Fi and decent bathrooms. But if you plan to stay here, don't expect peaceful, quiet nights.

Spondylus Campground

Address: Cap. Manuel Pineda 61, Fundo Legal, 23940 Guerrero Negro, B.C.S., Mexico

Phone Number: +52 615 159 7342

GPS Coordinates: 27.9722, -114.0204

Price Range: $25 USD

Spondylus campground is a nice, newer campground that pretty much caters to dry campers. There is no water and electricity hookup and the water pressure in showers is very low. But the Wi-Fi speed is excellent.

Moreover, it is pretty safe and the owners are very friendly. Also note that the entrance is difficult to maneuver and this is not the best option for larger RVs.

Best Boondocking /Alternative Camping Options

Ojo de Liebre (Scammon's Lagoon)

Guerrero Negro does not have much to offer. But nearby Ojo de Liebre, on Scammon's Lagoon just to the south of Guerrero Negro, is a great way to get away from the crowd. Follow a paved/dirt road through the salt flats and end up at the lagoon.

There is a small fee to camp here and coyotes have been known to be quite brave. But you can drive down the road as far as you and/or your vehicle will permit to find solace along the water. During whale-watching season this is the perfect way to combine camping with whale-watching tours offered at the restaurant.

Dunas de la Soledad

On the north side of Guerrero Negro you can find lots of boondocking opportunities around the sand dunes. You'll turn west at the airport and follow the paved road until it turns to dirt. Then follow various tracks back toward the sea until you find the spot that's perfect for you. There is no fee here, so pack out what you bring in. And know that the weather here is generally cooler and cloudier than in other parts of Baja.

San Ignacio

San Ignacio is a fertile oasis located in Mulege municipality, 90 miles (150 km) south of Guerrero Negro. If you're not looking for it, you'll miss the turnoff from Highway 1 and continue driving south. However, San Ignacio is the first place south of Guererro Negro worth your time - even if only for one night.

Of all of the small towns in Baja, this is one of our favorites as it has an element of being trapped in time. The town is a true desert oasis surrounded by beautiful palm and citrus orchards, sitting in the center of the hot Baja desert among cacti and volcanic boulders.

As you branch off the highway you'll leave the desert behind and drop into the lush palm oasis with the spring-fed San Ignacio river running adjacent to the road. The small, quiet river feeds the residents and all the orchards in the town and provides visitors an opportunity to kayak or paddleboard with a stunning view of Cerro Colorado.

As you approach the town itself you'll enter on cobblestone streets that lead to a small plaza at the center of town. Here, at the heart of San Ignacio, you'll find a handful of restaurants, street food vendors and shops that surround the plaza. But what will draw your attention immediately is the large mission and verdant garden at one end of the plaza.

Jesuits planted the palm gardens in 1728 and also built the famous mission. By far the most popular attraction in town, the historic and iconic Mision San Ignacio was built between 1778 and 1786 by Juan Bautista Luyando, a Jesuit. The church is constructed completely from volcanic rock and remains almost entirely intact from its original construction.

The peaceful town hustles and bustles between December to April when the nearby Laguna San Ignacio is filled with grey whales and visitors of all sorts use the town as a staging area both for whale excursions and other activities in the surrounding area.

Moreover, in the extreme heat of July, the traditional festival of San Ignacio is held to honor the death and life of the founder of the Jesuit order, Saint Ignatius of Loyola.

Things to Do in San Ignacio

San Ignacio is among the most beautiful small towns in Baja California Sur. The palm oasis is incredibly inviting and you will feel time slow down as soon as you begin walking around the plaza.

So, whether you are an adventure lover, a history buff or just want to live life a bit slowly, San Ignacio will keep you entertained.

Here are the best things to do in San Ignacio.

Walk Through the Mision San Ignacio

Mission San Ignacio is a historic building reflecting the craftsmanship of Cochimi Indians. It is the place that Cochimi called Kadacaaman, which was discovered in 1716.

The mission is made from 4-feet wide blocks of rocks collected from the nearby volcanoes. In addition to a remarkably beautiful exterior, the mission has an interior that reflects the splendor and solitude of an ancient sanctuary. Decorated with carved stone, wood and oil paintings with gold finishing, it is considered one of the most charming missions in Baja California.

Moreover, the church has barely changed over the years due to its solid construction. And it remains an active church with services of all kinds held regularly.

Visit the Cave Paintings

Another great activity in San Ignacio is visiting the cave paintings in the San Francisco de la Sierra mountains. There are multiple caves including La Natividad, El Parral, Cueva de la Serpiente, la Cuevona, Cueva del Raton, Cueva Pintada and El Brinco.

Deer and human paintings are the most significant and recognizable figures. You will also see some paintings of mountain lions and scenes depicting critical events in history.

You cannot visit the cave paintings on your own and will instead need to hire a licensed guide. Cave painting trips range from full-day to multiple-day excursions. Depending on which caves you visit, the path can be quite difficult and your guide will have mules to take you into the mountains.

Hang out with Locals in the Public Plaza

The plaza is an excellent spot to sit back, relax and interact with the locals. The beautiful park is a popular picnic spot. The Indian Laurel shades it, and there are tacos, ice cream and cold drinks stands surrounding the plaza.

There are a couple of grocery stores nearby and you can also bring food from any of the nearby restaurants to enjoy in the plaza. While playing with our dogs in the plaza once we ended up in a spirited game of soccer (futbol) with a dozen local kids whose laughter we'll never forget!

Go Whale Watching in Laguna San Ignacio

Laguna San Ignacio is among the best whale-watching areas in the Baja Peninsula. It is the only undeveloped lagoon in the region, lying around 40 miles (65 km) southwest of San Ignacio via a mixture of paved and very unfriendly dirt roads.

The road to the lagoon is not paved beyond the town limits, so having a 4x4 vehicle is the best option for an easy and safe ride.

There are just over half a dozen tour companies arranging whale watching tours in the lagoon. But do know that you will need to book tours several weeks in advance during the peak of the season (February and March).

Campgrounds in San Ignacio

Rice and Beans RV Park

Address:	Av. Deborah Wayne Carretera Transpeninsular, San lino, 23930 San Ignacio, B.C.S., Mexico
Website:	https://sites.google.com/site/ricardoriceandbeans/
Phone Number:	+52 615 154 0283
GPS Coordinates:	27.2989, -112.9043
Price Range:	$20 - 25 USD

(Electric is 20 amp only)

Rice and Beans is a nice 30-campsite RV park with a pool and a restaurant. It has full hookups and is big-rig friendly. But the camp is not as scenic or centrally located as other campgrounds in San Ignacio.

The restrooms and showers are decent and overall this is a great place to camp if you're looking to just spend one night and move on.

El Padrino RV Park

Phone Number:	+52 615 161 6888, +52 615 154 0089
GPS Coordinates:	27.2857, -112.9013
Price Range:	$10 - 12 USD

El Padrino is the closest campground to the town, within walking distance to the town plaza. It is a nice affordable campground with decent Wi-Fi, toilets, hot showers and 20 amp electric hookups.

Sites are spacious and the campground is big rig friendly. Although you won't have full hookups, there is water and a dump station available if needed.

Campos Los Petates

GPS Coordinates:	27.2966, -112.8985
Price Range:	$9 - 12 USD

Campos Los Petates is a wonderful campground located at the edge of the lagoon and surrounded by beautiful palm trees. It is an affordable dry camping site with a decent bathroom and hot showers.

The campground is only 5 minutes away from the center of town. Note that the entrance is a bit tight because of the palm trees. But that adds to the ambiance of the lush oasis campground.

All sites are dry camping and mostly shady. But they're also all located along the lagoon. There is no WiFi, but the cell service is pretty decent.

Best Boondocking /Alternative Camping Options

Plaza Publica

There is no finer boondocking in all of Baja that provides as much opportunity to experience an evening in a quintessential Mexican town than at the central plaza in San Ignacio. You can literally park on the street and spend the evening worry-free.

Get out and enjoy whatever festivities are taking place in the plaza, pick up a bite to eat at everything from sit-down restaurants to taco stands and fall asleep in one of the quietest places you'll find.

It is likely that you won't be the only one spending the night in the plaza. This is a great place to make friends, both with locals and fellow travelers. And we're confident you'll enjoy your time in the town.

Laguna San Ignacio

Laguna San Ignacio is one of Baja's primary winter sanctuaries for the Pacific Grey Whale. In this protected lagoon, young females give birth to their calves between December to April and prepare them for the long journey to the northern waters in summer. Here you can "pet," kiss and even hug the gentle giants. It is truly an experience nobody should miss.

The lagoon is located in the Mulege Municipality of Baja California Sur about 35 miles (60 km) southwest of the beautiful date oasis of San Ignacio.

The road is not easy to navigate and requires 4x4 in parts, making it a quieter, and less-visited gem in Baja if you can get there. A paved road is in the works, so things are bound to get better soon, for what it's worth.

Laguna San Ignacio is huge. It stretches about 15 miles (25 km) into the desert and has a maximum width of around 5 miles (8 km).

As a UNESCO World Heritage and UN Biosphere Reserve for migratory birds, Laguna San Ignacio is the only undeveloped lagoon in Baja and you have to book a tour or make advance reservations to reach your destination.

Most of the lagoon's permanent inhabitants are fishermen who are permitted to fish the waters all the way up until the whales begin to arrive. As the grey whales are protected, all fishing shuts down and the fishermen convert their services and boats into whale-watching tours.

In addition to grey whales, the Laguna San Ignacio is a feeding ground for endangered and elusive Pronghorn Antelope and four species of sea turtles. There are numerous Bottlenose dolphin pods and California sea lion colonies scattered throughout the lagoon as well.

Moreover, you will find many birds, including herons, ospreys, and white egrets feasting on the bountiful fish populations in the lagoon. On some occasions, you will also see some coyotes exploring the cactus-studded desert.

Whale Watching Camps in Laguna San Ignacio

Laguna San Ignacio is not very developed and only a handful of whale-watching organizations, nearly all dubbed "eco" in nature, have set up seasonal camps along the southeastern edge of the lagoon.

Because the road in is so difficult, most offer private transportation and on-site accommodations to make the trip out to the lagoon more worthwhile.

There are a few excellent whale-watching camps in Laguna San Ignacio. The camps provide comfortable and eco-friendly accommodations and arrange whale-watching trips. Moreover, the experts also help you learn more about the local wildlife and history.

Here are the best whale-watching camps in Laguna San Ignacio.

Antonio's Ecotours

Antonio's Ecotours is a family-run camp that offers rustic, but comfortable accommodations on the shore of the lagoon. One of the region's whale-watching pioneers, Antonio is a hospitable host who, along with his wife "Yaki" go out of their way to share their home with you and ensure your stay is as memorable as it can be.

Camp in rustic cabins, eat freshly caught and prepared seafood and enjoy beautiful sunrises and sunsets during your stay.

Baja Expeditions

Baja Expeditions is one of the best and oldest Whale watching camps in Laguna San Ignacio. It was established 50 years ago, and now they are a leader in eco-adventures throughout Baja. Baja Expeditions have some of the most luxurious tents.

And they have flexible tour plans with an average of three whale watching sessions per day. They also give naturalist presentations every morning to increase your knowledge about whales and local wildlife.

MAS Luxury Wilderness Escapes

MAS Luxury is another excellent whale-watching camp. They have great food with all the luxury amenities, including hot showers, comfortable beds, clean bathrooms, a sitting area and exceptional service.

They also offer multiple whale watching sessions daily. And you can also opt between hiking, mountain biking, bird watching and visiting the nearby salt flats.

Santa Rosalia

Santa Rosalia is a different kind of seaside Baja town, one that most travelers breeze through on their way north or south. It is built around a copper mine established by the French, so you will see a lot of French influence in the buildings and living style of the people, particularly in the Iglesia de Santa Barbara, an iron church designed by Alexandre-Gustave Eiffel.

The copper mine was closed in 1954, but the remains of mining equipment are scattered around the town giving it an almost ghost town feel (were it not for all the people and new businesses built along the main road in town).

Santa Rosalia is around a one-hour drive from San Ignacio on breathtaking steep curves around the sandstone cliffs along the stunning blue Gulf of California. This is one area you will want to pay attention to the grade of the road, which is not marked.

From the north, you will be going on a mostly steep downhill on your way into Santa Rosalia. The reverse is true on your way back north. Be mindful of your brakes, engine and transmission as you wind your way into Santa Rosalia.

Santa Rosalia itself has a colorful history, first written by Cochimi Indians on the walls and caves of nearby mountains. They lived there for thousands of years fishing the fertile waters and living among the stunning landscape and vegetation.

The second chapter was written by the French when small green copper nuggets were discovered in Santa Rosalia. They planned to start mining for copper in El Boleo. The French shipped tons of construction material, steel, engines, rails and railway cars to the bay from Europe and developed hundreds of miles of tunnels, a railroad, a pier and a smelting factory.

The mined ores were taken to Washington to be refined. In the 1950s, the 60-year-old structure was failing, and production fell drastically. So, El Boleo had to be shut down. In 1954, the mine stopped production, and the French left a fascinating reminder of the riches and loss throughout mining history.

Things to Do in Santa Rosalia

Although the town is not a top destination in Baja, there are some interesting things to do in San Rosalia. The primary tourist attractions include the Iglesia de Santa Barbara, traditional authentic French baguettes and pastries and the Museum of Mining Industry.

Tour the Iglesia de Santa Barbara

The Iglesia de Santa Barbara, or Santa Barbara Church, is the highlight of the small seaside town. It was designed by Alexandre-Gustave Eiffel, the architect of the Eiffel Tower in Paris, in 1880.

Carlos La Frogue acquired the church and individually shipped metal plates from Europe. Then the church was reconstructed in Santa Rosalia in 1897. The beautiful church sits right in the middle of the city and is easily accessible to everyone.

Visit the Museum of Mining History

Most of the factories and industrial facilities were dismantled after the French left Santa Rosalia and were not accessible to the public. But the main mining office of La Boleo has been converted into an industrial museum. It has a great collection of some of the machines with a detailed history of the mining industry of the region and time.

Take the Ferry to the Mainland

Santa Rosalia has a small ferry terminal you can board for a real adventure to mainland Mexico from Baja. The Ferry leaves on Wednesday, Friday, and Sunday. The journey enables you to experience the stunning blue ocean of Santa Rosalia... that is IF the ferry is operational. This ferry is notorious for not running according to any schedule.

Eat at the Panaderia El Boleo

Panaderia El Boleo is a French bakery in downtown Santa Rosalia. It is quite popular among travelers and residents alike. They serve authentic, delicious French bread, pastries and other baked goods.

Campgrounds in Santa Rosalia

As Santa Rosalia is not a top destination for travelers, there is very little by way of camping in or around town. In fact, there is really only one place that is worth the effort to stay in if you want to spend time in the area.

San Lucas Cove

Address: Ejido San Lucas Rv park San Lucas Cove, 23911 Ejido San Lucas, B.C.S., Mexico

Phone Number: +52 615 103 6766

GPS Coordinates: 27.2191, -112.2146

Price Range: $12 USD

San Lucas Cove is an affordable campground just 10 minutes away from Santa Rosalia. The beachfront RV park is built near a small restaurant and a store is within walking distance.

There is no electricity and sewage, water is acceptable and the bathrooms and showers are pretty worn out. Further, the campground bay is often full of stingrays, so taking a swim is not a good idea here.

Mulege

The palm oasis of Mulege is located on the peaceful coastline of the Sea of Cortez. The colorful town has a stunning green landscape to provide a stark contrast to the rugged deserts. Mulege lies 40 miles (65 km) south of Santa Rosalia and around 12 hours away from the US/Mexico border.

The peaceful town has a mild climate with waters teeming with fish and is the jumping-off point for all of the Bahia de Concepcion beaches. For these reasons and more, Mulege is one of the top spots for ex-pats and travelers alike.

Local Indians lived in Mulege for thousands of years because of the abundance of fresh water and the fertile Sea of Cortez. You will find many cave paintings in the nearby mountains of Sierra de Guadalupe.

Mulege was most recently discovered by the Jesuit father Juan Maria de Salvatierra who founded Mission Santa Rosalia de Mulege in 1705. The town retains much of its historical charm with colonial architecture and cobblestone streets.

Mulege's official name is "Heroica Mulege," awarded after the Mexican-American war of 1846-48. Americans tried to take over the pacific coastline of Baja, California. But the people of Mulege and nearby areas gathered and successfully defeated the Americans.

As a result, the town got the title of Heroica Mulege. To this day, there are quite a few locals who will be quick to remind you of the time they beat the Americans in Mulege.

In addition to fishing, agriculture is a major part of the local economy. The sound weather, fertile soil and rich water supply from the Mulege River have supported agriculture for years. At first, it was limited to date orchards like nearby San Ignacio. But now Mulege boasts many tropical fruits including oranges, bananas, limes and mangoes.

Mulege is the gateway to Bahia Concepcion, one of the largest and most popular bays in Baja known for its stunning white sand beaches, beautiful coves and crystal clear water. It is an excellent spot for swimming, snorkeling, scuba diving, sportfishing and many other watersports.

Mulege also has a beautiful Mission developed by Father Francisco Escalante in 1766. You will also find a defunct prison that is now a museum and boasts some spectacular history. It was a one-of-a-kind prison and stayed operational until 1975. Moreover, ancient cave paintings of Cochimí Indians are not far from the city.

Things to Do in Mulege

The small oasis town in the center of Baja is full of beauty and tranquility. With clear blue sea and sandy beaches nearby, quaint colonial buildings in town and lots of history and culture, there are many reasons why you should consider a stop in Mulege.

Here are the best things to do in Mulege.

Go Fishing

Mulege is extremely popular for sportfishing and water sports. Residents have been fishing in this area along the Sea of Cortez for thousands of years. It is a fish-rich ocean filled with many beautiful and exotic fish because of its perfect temperature, created by the mixture of warm southern and cold northern currents.

The ideal temperature enables the growth of a variety of species. Moreover, various migratory fish are also found around the year.

You can easily book a sportfishing tour in town. Or head to any tourist bar and strike up a conversation with any ex-pat that will fill you in on who can take you out on the water.

Explore the Mission Santa Rosalia de Mulege

The Mission Santa Rosalia de Mulege is the second oldest mission in Baja. It is located not too far from the town center across the Rio Mulege. The mission sits atop a hill and provides stunning views of palm date oasis and surrounding hillsides.

There is a small dam below the mission that you can walk across. It was built by the missionaries and local Indians to irrigate the local crops. The mission serves as a catholic church for the locals and visitors are allowed to enter during specific hours.

Visit Bahia Concepcion

Bahia Concepcion is the most popular tourist attraction near Mulege. It is a huge bay on the Sea of Cortez that boasts miles and miles of beautiful beaches and shoreline. Some of the beaches are quieter than others. But all of them are pleasant and worth a stop if you have the time.

The water along the bay tends to be calm, pleasant and cool, allowing you to relax and enjoy snorkeling, paddleboarding or kayaking, fishing and sunbathing. Beaches like El Requeson and Playa Santispac are the most visited beaches.

But there are plenty of other beaches, all within an hour of Mulege. You'll want to read on to the next section for more specific information about camping along Bahia Concepcion.

Wander Through the Old Prison / Museo de Mulege

The prison was built in 1907 as the only jail without bars. During the day, prisoners were permitted to leave the jail and work routine jobs, be with their families, and return to the prison by 6 pm. Escape attempts were rare because Mulege was a very isolated area with a long desert on every side of the town.

It was operational until 1975 when it was then converted into a museum. While not the most spectacular museum, you can appreciate the view the inmates and guards had looking out over the Mulege River from the top of the hill.

Find the San Borjitas Cave Paintings

If you're a fan of exploring local history, you'll have a good time heading out to San Borjitas cave paintings. These paintings were discovered by Jesuits and are estimated to be 7500 years old. Although Cochimi Indians have been living in the area for thousands of years, no one knows who drew those paintings of women, warriors, whales, deer and fish.

The caves are around a 90-minute ride on a bumpy road. The entrance fee is not much, but you will have to have a 4x4 vehicle and a guide.

Volunteer in Mulege

Casa Hogar

Casa Hogar is an orphanage in Mulege that works with kids in the town and surrounding areas. Although not all of the children are orphans, the organization caters to assisting children of all ages and backgrounds. Although donations are typically the preferred method of assisting if you reach out you may be able to volunteer with specific projects, particularly if you have special skills and abilities.

Email: sarl780424@hotmail.com
Facebook: https://www.facebook.com/casahogarelaltisimo

PAW

PAW clinic, located just a few minutes south of Mulege, is a great place to volunteer if you enjoy helping out with animals. As a gringo volunteer veterinary clinic, it operates between November and April and treats hundreds of different animals.

Depending on your background, you may be able to do some hands-on helping at the clinic in addition to general administrative duties. You can also support the organization financially or by having your animals treated here at a fraction of the cost of the US or Canada but where your payment will subsidize local care.

Email: mulegepaw@yahoo.com
Phone: +52 615 103 4049
Website: https://pawclinic.wordpress.com/

Campgrounds in Mulege

At present, there is only one campground located in Mulege and a handful of others located across the river. So if you want to camp near town within walking or biking distance, you'll want to go with Huerta Don Chano. Otherwise, if you don't mind a short drive into town you have a few options.

Huerta Don Chano RV Park

Address:	Playa, Loma Azul, 23900 Heroica Mulegé, B.C.S., Mexico
Phone Number:	+52 615 107 5851
GPS Coordinates:	26.8981, -111.9749
Price Range:	$15 - 20 USD

Huerta Don Chano is a pleasant campground filled with fruit trees and palm grass. It is around a mile away from the town center headed out toward the lighthouse at the end of the Sea of Cortez.

The campground has a nice restaurant and it doesn't take long to walk or bike into town. We love this campground because most of the sites are sectioned off by lush papaya, mango and citrus trees that the owners of the park usually allow you to pick yourselves during the season. Moreover, the showers are hot and the staff is as friendly as it comes in Baja.

Note, if you have a Class A or a large 5th wheel or travel trailer you will want to find another option. You will likely be able to make the drive through town to the campground. But getting out of town requires one very tight turn that would not be very feasible for larger rigs.

Villa Maria Isabel RV Park

Address:	Carr. Transpeninsular km 134, 23900 Heroica Mulegé, B.C.S., Mexico
Phone Number:	+52 811 208 7586
GPS Coordinates:	26.8969, -111.9639
Price Range:	$15 - 25 USD

Villa Maria Isabel is a big-rig friendly campground just a few minutes away from the town on the opposite side of the Mulege River. The beachfront campsite has everything you need. The owner is very helpful and the RV park has a small swimming pool.

They also rent kayaks and snorkeling gear and can help arrange fishing trips if you are interested. The campsites are on dirt. But the campground itself is very well kept and inviting.

Hotel Serenidad

Address:	Frente a la Playa s/n, El Cachano, 23900 Heroica Mulegé, B.C.S., Mexico
Website:	http://www.serenidad.com.mx/
Phone Number:	+52 615 153 0530
GPS Coordinates:	26.8976, -111.9585
Price Range:	$20 - 25 USD

Hotel Serenidad is basically a hotel with seven campsites. They have a great pool for relaxing and all the amenities you need from a practical standpoint. Showers are by the pool and bathrooms are clean.

Best Boondocking /Alternative Camping Options

Faro de Mulege

By far the best place to boondock in Mulege is at the beach in front of the lighthouse. To reach this spot, you'll have to come through town and head out to the very end of the road that leads past Don Chanos. The cement road will turn to dirt for the last mile or so and then turn to rocks as you reach the water's edge.

It is likely you won't be the only one here. And if you arrive during the weekend, don't expect it to be quiet as this beach is popular among locals.

There are a few palapas you can park next to. Or simply find the best view and pull over for the evening. There is great fishing all around the lighthouse and sunsets and sunrises are not much better than here.

Bay of Concepcion

Bahia Concepcion is one of the most desirable places to camp in Baja. In fact, we've known many travelers who have never made it further south along Highway 1 than the Bay of Concepcion.

They fell in love with the sandy beaches, sunshine and warm saltwater of the bay and never looked back. And we have seen many first-timers extend their vacations to thoroughly experience the bay's charm and tranquility.

If you follow Highway 1 south out of Mulege for around half an hour you'll reach the first of a handful of beaches along the bay.

The bay itself offers 20 miles of some of the most spectacular coastal scenery in the Baja California Peninsula. A dozen formal sandy beaches are scattered between rocky points and coves and offer travelers places to camp for around $10 - 15 USD per night.

Bahia Concepcion used to be the fishing capital of Baja. It had all sorts of incredible fish in abundance and celebrities used to fly into Mulege to head into the bay for some spectacular population.

But overfishing has significantly depleted the fish situation in the region. And while it's still possible to land a Rooster Fish or triggerfish just offshore or near one of the many small islands, the catch can be few and far between.

But there are a lot of things to do in Bahia Concepcion, mostly involving relaxing or watersports. The huge beach has facilities for all sorts of watersport activities, including kayaking and paddleboarding, snorkeling, diving and boating. Occasionally it is windy enough to enjoy wind sports such as kiteboarding, windsurfing or sailing.

If you're looking to stay active on the water or are simply looking for a quiet place to relax along the beach, Bahia Concepcion plays host to the iconic Baja beaches.

Things to Do in Bahia Concepcion

Bahia Concepcion is probably one of the most beautiful areas in Baja. The stunning beaches, beautiful landscape, and clear sea keep us returning year after year.

Here are the best things to do in Bahia Concepcion.

Enjoy Watersports

Like all the beaches in Baja, Bahia Concepcion has all the offerings to enjoy watersports. In fact, it is considered a paradise for campers, snorkelers, and kayakers, because of the calm and peaceful bay creates an ideal environment for these activities. Moreover, rare but sudden winds also allow windsurfers and kiteboarders to race across the bay.

Buenaventura, Playa Requeson, Playa Santispac, and coves around the lighthouse are the best places for snorkeling, paddleboarding and kayaking. You can also find whale sharks seasonally on a variety of beaches via boat, kayak or paddleboard.

Go Hiking

The 20-mile bay has many hiking trails that you can walk to experience the panoramic views of Bahia Concepcion. Here are a few of the quick and easy hikes along the bay, all starting at the beach indicated.

Playa Los Cocos

You can take a short hike on the northern end of the beach to go up and over a nearby hill. From there you will look down upon and be able to meet up with Playa Escondido.

Playa El Burro

Here is a short, steep 900 feet hike on the hill north of Playa El Burro.

The trail is clearly visible from the beach. Standing on the rocky spine will give excellent views of the bay.

Playa el Coyote
The hike starts from the south end of the beach and takes you to the top of a small hill near a cove. The longer walk to a cove is also possible if you want.

Burro Cove Hike
Burro is a stunning cove in Bahia Concepcion. The hike is relatively short, following the old road separating Burro beach from Coyote.

Just Relax
Bahia Concepcion is a great place to sit back, relax and live at a slow pace. The modern amenities (and distractions) are not there and you literally have to go out of your way to get to the closest restaurants and entertainment.

In fact, many of these beaches have grown into seasonal ex-pat communities by those who prefer the warm winter nights and the company of new and old friends.

Beaches in Bahia Concepcion
While each beach deserves its own write-up, the following beaches are the most accessible and popular among travelers. You will pay a small fee for basic amenities, such as trash cans, pit toilets and water delivery.

Some of these beaches offer restaurants and/or small stores. But plan to stock up in Mulege if traveling from the north, or Loreto if coming from the south.

The following beaches are listed from north to south as you travel from Mulege to Loreto.

Playa Santispac

Playa Santispac is the first beach and is easy to access through Highway 1. The sheer breathtaking beauty has made this a haven for snowbirds. The calm water of the beach is excellent for snorkeling, kayaking and paddleboarding.

This is the largest and most big-rig-friendly of the beaches listed. So if you have a Class A or large travel trailer you may want to look no further than Playa Santispac for camping.

There are a few restaurants on the beach, a small store and the opportunity to purchase very scattered satellite WiFi if you must connect to the world outside of Bahia Concepcion.

Playa la Escondida

Playa Escondida, as its name suggests, is a hidden beach accessible through a narrow rocky road not suitable for low clearance or long rigs. It is one of the more difficult beaches to reach, and thus you will not find many tourists there. The beautiful beach is an ideal spot for snorkeling and relaxing.

Playa Los Cocos

Playa Los Cocos is just a short drive south of Playa Escondida and offers a slightly easier path to its sandy beaches. The turn-off is not always well-marked and, like most beaches on Bahia Concepcion, you'll follow a suspect dirt road that is always subject to changing conditions. But you can have a bit of isolation here.

Playa El Burro

Playa El Burro or Donkey Cove Beach is located just before El Coyote. It is not the most beautiful beach as most of the cove is taken up by permanent residents. However, there is a free camping area at the southern end of the beach. And Playa El Burro has a restaurant if you get tired of cooking.

Playa El Coyote

Playa El Coyote is a semi-gated beach that is popular among both locals and campers alike. Most campsites include a palapa and you will find that vendors will come by daily to offer everything from fresh water and fruit to kayak rentals and blankets.

The beach is divided by a narrow, rocky stretch of road that can be intimidating to larger rigs. However, it is one of the more popular beaches for ex-pats, which is both a draw and a deterrent for many travelers. Like other beaches, don't expect anything by way of amenities - other than some rudimentary outhouses and plenty of sunshine to keep your solar system happy.

Playa El Buenaventura

Playa El Buenaventura is located about halfway down Bahia Concepcion. What is billed mostly as private residences and businesses, the beach offers the opportunity to camp away from other RVs.

The beach has facilities for kayaking and paddleboarding and you can usually find quality information about fishing in the bay by asking around. The restaurant at the beach also serves some pretty decent food.

Playa El Requeson

Playa El Requeson is the last easily accessible beach of Bahia Concepcion, famous for its unique landscape. In fact, the road to reach the beach is paved off Highway 1, unlike any other beach along the bay.

Known for the spit of land visible at low tide, which is then covered with water as the tide rises, Playa El Requeson is literally picture-perfect. Because of its reputation, it receives a lot of daily tourist traffic.

But at night the beach is very quiet and the night sky is typically filled with stars. Like the other beaches, there are suspect pit toilets and no other amenities.

Playa La Perla

Playa La Perla is a gem of a beach not easily accessible for most RVs. Because it is difficult to reach and offers fewer formal campsites than its neighbors, Playa La Perla feels far more remote and uninhabited. There is a small sandy beach here. But much of Playa La Perla is a rocky shoreline not as ideal for watersports as the other beaches.

Playa Armenta

Playa Armenta is the beach furthest south and arguably the most difficult to reach. You can see the beach from the highway at the end of a steep descent suitable only for smaller RVs, vans and car-camping vehicles.

It is not much developed, but some pit toilets and palapas exist. But because it is not as popular, you can stay there to swim in crystal clear water and enjoy the breathtaking views sometimes all by yourself.

Loreto

Loreto is the kind of town in Baja that most travelers either love or hate. It has all of the modern amenities, both for camping and living. Plus, with an influx of ex-pats, the town is becoming more and more comfortable by American standards.

Loreto itself is the oldest permanent settlement in Baja, founded in 1697 when Juan Maria De Salvatierra began the still operational Mision de Nuestra Senora de Loreto Conch. The town is historically rich with significant native and Spanish influence.

Today it is a popular tourist destination and serves as the regional cultural and economic center. It also has an airport that regularly receives international flights, making Loreto a leading second home alternative to Cabo San Lucas for Americans flying in.

Loreto is getting popular for being a quiet and peaceful tourist destination. The modern city has many landmark projects and buildings, such as an 18-hole golf course and a nice tennis club.

Also, the National Maritime Park, a World Heritage Site, has a huge impact on growing the eco-tourism industry in the area. The park is home to many beautiful marine species including killer whales, blue whales, sea lions, dolphins, sea urchins, starfish and a variety of shellfish.

Nearby, San Javier Mission is the best-preserved mission in the whole of Mexico. It is an hour from the city, located in the rugged mountains of Sierra de la Giganta.

Loreto is an excellent sportfishing destination. It is a popular tourist attraction and the primary source of income for a large portion of the local population. You can catch various fish like red snapper and seabass all year long.

Moreover, the waters have a significant blue whale population, giving you an opportunity to witness the largest animal on the planet in person.

Things to Do in Loreto

From reliving the town's foundation in Mission Nuestra Senora de Loreto to snorkeling or paddleboarding with the ocean's gentle creatures, Loreto has something for everyone.

Here are the things to do in Loreto.

Take a Stroll in the Historic Downtown

Loreto is a small town with tons of nearby natural attractions. But if you are in the town, you don't want to miss a walk through the downtown area. The city center is known for its tree-lined cobblestone archways, colorful buildings, cafes and restaurants.

Although Loreto's Malecon is not as popular as other towns in Baja, it is definitely worth a stroll as well. Plaza Civica is home to Loreto town hall and a space for events and festivals. The plaza is surrounded by some good cafes and restaurants.

Head Out to Coronado Island

Coronado Island sits in the Sea of Cortez, just 25 minutes away from Loreto. It is part of the National Maritime Park and is home to sea lions, many fish and aquatic birds like blue-footed boobies. People visit the island to enjoy the serene views, relax and take a dip in turquoise waters.

Coronado Island has excellent land and sea activities for those looking for a unique adventure. You can snorkel, paddleboard, kayak and swim around the beautiful seawater. On land, you can participate in bird-watching tours, hiking and sunbathing.

Certain tours will plan multi-day adventures on the island and you can only camp there with a special permit.

Catch a Peek at the Giant Blue Whales

Loreto is one of the few places in the world where you can have a reasonable expectation to see a blue whale in nature. From February to March, they stay in the calm waters of Loreto Bay. But know that Blue Whales are not as interactive as grey whales, so finding them can be slightly tricky.

Many tour operators offer a full-day whale watching experience to increase the chance that you see one. These tours leave in the morning and stay in the area for several hours, where whales are known to be hanging around.

Just don't be disappointed if you don't see a single one of the mystical creatures during your time on the water.

Go Sportfishing

Another great place to hook a prize fish, Loreto is known for its sportfishing and is arguably the biggest tourist attraction to the area. Finding a fishing boat is not difficult. You will find many tour operators and freelance captains offering their services on one of the many pangas in the marina.

In summer, you may be able to hook giant marlin and sailfish. While the winter season tends to bring yellowtail, dorado and a few others. Loreto waters are also home to seabass and snapper, which are relatively easy to catch bottom fishing.

Visit San Javier Mission

The San Javier Mission is located around an hour away from Loreto and is considered one of the best-preserved missions in Mexico. The construction started in 1699 and was then abandoned because of the water supply. After a few unsuccessful attempts, it was shifted a few miles away near a natural water spring.

The mission is easily accessible by car or small to mid-sized RV Some tour operators also organize cycling tours from Loreto to San Javier Mission.

Hike Tabor Canyon

Loreto is surrounded by the towering red rock mountains and cliffs of the Sierra de la Giganta Mountain range. The beautiful Tabor Canyon hike is a gateway to stunning views and spectacular rock formations.

The trailhead is around 20 minutes away from the city center, and you can go as far into the canyon as you want. It is not very difficult, but you may have to climb huge boulders to go ahead in some places.

Paddleboard or Kayak in the Peaceful Water of Loreto Bay

Loreto Bay is a perfect place for kayaking and paddleboarding. You can rent paddleboards and kayaks at the beach and can embark on one-day and multi-day tours with different guides and operators.

While the water nearby Loreto is not as spectacular as it is in some places throughout Baja, the wildlife is abundant and you are almost guaranteed to see dolphin if you paddle far enough.

Campgrounds in Loreto

Camping in Loreto can be tricky as several of the RV parks are located on pedestrian streets in the center of town. But what is great about these campgrounds is that you are literally in the middle of town so you are within walking distance of everything.

Riviera del Mar RV Park

Address:	Francisco. I. Madero Loreto, Baja California Sur, Mexico 23880
Phone Number:	+52 613 135 0718
GPS Coordinates:	26.0175, -111.3459
Price Range:	$10 - 20 USD

Riviera del Mar RV Park is a central place in Loreto. It has around 25 sites with some flat patches for pitching tents and parking small campervans. The ground has a nice common sitting area with electricity plugs and a sink to wash dishes.

The bathrooms also tend to be nice and clean. This is your best bet if you have a large RV and want to spend time in Loreto.

Romanita RV Park

Address:	Salvatierra 4, entre Callejón Romanita y Plaza Central Loreto, BCS, Mexico
Website:	https://romanitarvpark.com/
Phone Number:	+52 613 121 2160
GPS Coordinates:	26.0111, -111.3407
Price Range:	$12 - 20 USD

Romanita is another excellent RV park located directly in the city center. It has all the amenities, including full hookups, laundry, a clean bathroom, showers and security. However, Romanita is not suitable for big RVs.

We advise that you call in advance before trying to drive to Romanita RV Park as you will need to follow pedestrian walkways, which is intimidating if you aren't certain of where you are going!

El Moro RV Park

Address:	Centro, 23880 Loreto, Baja California Sur, Mexico
Website:	https://www.facebook.com/ElMoroHotel/
Phone Number:	+52 011 135 0542
GPS Coordinates:	26.01166, -111.34137
Price Range:	$10 - 20 USD

El Moro RV Park is a small campground in the heart of the downtown area on the other side of an alley from Romanita. It is an affordable campground with electricity, sewer and water hookups.

Otherwise, this place is not for everyone. The bathrooms are not the best and showers are known to only be hot during the day when you are likely to be out exploring Loreto. Moreover, Wi-Fi performance is satisfactory and it is also not very big-rig friendly.

Once again, call in advance as you will need to drive through pedestrian streets to reach El Moro.

San Juanico (Scorpion Bay)

San Juanico, most known for its encompassing Scorpion Bay, is a small fishing village located on the coast of the Pacific Ocean. The village has a population of just a few hundred people, although the transient population explodes anytime there are waves to surf in Scorpion Bay.

American surfers noticed the incredible waves in the 1970s and afterward San Juanico grew with a reputation of being one of the best surfing spots in the world.

San Juanico is typically a peaceful and slow village with a lot of artists and those people looking to escape the development of many of the other popular towns in Baja. But as the town is often on most Baja 1000 race routes, everything seems to move faster during the race as many teams and spectators camp in the village.

Moreover, fishing is another popular tourist attraction. Scorpion bay has some of the best fish in Baja including seabass, yellowtail and Corvina.

There are two ways to reach San Juanico. Firstly, you can start from San Ignacio Lagoon and arrive in San Juanico a few hours later via the mandatory 4WD "North Route." The path is unpaved, unmarked and bumpy.

But having driven this route with a caravan that had been making the trip for nearly 20 years, we don't recommend driving the North Route even with 4WD because it is very easy to get lost among the various paths and trails.

The second one is the South Route which requires you to drive into Ciudad Insurgentes before turning north toward La Purisima. This is the best route, as the road is paved all the way to San Juanico. But the drive is almost 7 hours longer than the North Route.

Things to Do in San Juanico

Scorpion Bay is a tiny fishing village, and there is not much to do except fishing and surfing in the Pacific Ocean.

Here are the things to do in San Juanico.

Go Surfing

San Juanico is often among the top 10 surfing spots in the world. During the right swell, the bay produces more than 6 break waves, allowing you to ride for what seems to be from one end of the bay to the other. The legendary point breaks make it an unforgettable surfing destination for every surfer.

However, when there are no waves the bay is incredibly calm and is more suited for other water activities such as kayaking, paddle boarding, fishing and boating.

Head Out Fishing

Like every Baja Bay, Scorpion Bay is also quite rich with diverse game fish. Local fishermen will take you on half-day fishing tours in the Pacific in their pangas. Ensure that you have all your supplies before embarking on the journey because some fishermen will not provide fishing poles or equipment.

Embrace the Art and Culture

San Juanico is not just about fishing, surfing and water activities. There is another side of tranquility, connecting with nature and stepping back in time. Local art, culture and tradition are displayed in Galleria la Cura.

And you'll find that most of the shops and stores in town are aesthetically pleasing and artistic in nature. There are also many opportunities to join yoga and meditation sessions at a variety of places in San Juanico.

Campgrounds in San Juanico

There are no formal campgrounds in San Juanico at present. As the town itself is still developing, as slowly as possible, there does not seem to be the infrastructure to support or justify a proper campground.

However, if you have 4WD and/or are comfortable driving on soft sand, you are welcome to camp anywhere on the beach along Scorpion Bay. Be mindful of the tides and weather and be certain you have the confidence to find your way out of the sand if you get stuck.

Best Boondocking /Alternative Camping Option

On the Beach

If you have the right vehicle and/or confidence in yourself, camping on the beach along Scorpion Bay is your best option. You'll leave town and drop down toward the sand where the local fishermen leave their boats.

Head back along the beach as far as you feel comfortable. Keep an eye on the tides. But even if the surf is up, it's likely you'll still find plenty of space to yourself.

La Paz

La Paz, the capital of Baja California Sur and the largest city in the southern state, is a remarkably calm and inviting city. Located on a bay within a bay, La Paz means "peace," and it is truly a peaceful place considering its size.

For this reason, it attracts visitors of all kinds and is a popular spot for ex-pats looking to combine modern amenities with authentic Mexican culture.

On our first visit, we were intimidated by the idea of spending any amount of time in or around a larger city. However, of all of the cities in Baja, La Paz is by far the safest and most welcoming with loads of fun things to do in the area.

The city is also home to several of the most beautiful beaches in Mexico - Balandra and Tecolote. Despite being a modern and the biggest city in Baja California Sur, it perfectly exhibits the old Baja charm. La Paz is a favorite destination for divers, golfers and sportfishing enthusiasts.

Geographically, La Paz is the fourth largest municipality in Mexico and boasts the largest population in Baja California Sur with over 250,000 people. It has an airport and a ferry terminal connecting the region with mainland Mexico and the rest of the world.

La Paz is undergoing a massive transformation. It is developing rapidly, particularly on the northeast end of the downtown. Moreover, there are several golf courses and high-end marinas full of very expensive yachts and sailboats.

In addition to construction, the art of La Paz is on another level. The city is filled with stunning street art, murals and urban art pieces depicting the cultural origin, indigenous people, and their relationship with the sea.

A walk along the Malecon will introduce you to all sorts of statues and art connecting the city with its natural and historical roots.

The La Paz municipality is also the land of stunning beaches. In fact, Balandra Beach is one of the most unique and picturesque beaches in the world. Thousands of people visit Balandra on any given day.

The white sandy beaches and crystal clear water invites visitors of all kinds to rest and relax, paddle and play in the water of the hourglass-shaped bay.

In addition to Balandra, there are other beaches where you can enjoy all the water activities, including swimming, snorkeling, scuba diving, fishing and kayaking. Playa Tecolote and Playa Pichilingue are two where you can camp on the beach and enjoy everything the southern end of Baja has to offer.

Like many other Baja towns, La Paz also hosts friendly whale sharks, grey whales, humpback, and blue whales from January through April. Whale sharks, in particular, are the main attraction in La Paz.

During winter and spring, female and juvenile whale sharks follow the warm water and food into the bay where they stay until migrating north in late spring. This is one of the few places in the world where you can leave the city on a tour boat and be in the water swimming with whale sharks within 30 minutes.

In addition to excellent water activities, La Paz is a great place for sandboarding in the El Mogote desert, mountain biking the nearby Sierra de la Laguna Mountains and hiking to lagoons and beautiful vistas along the water.

Things to Do in La Paz

The tropical desert, unspoiled beaches and fantastic wildlife make La Paz a great destination to explore. It has tons of activities for every person.

Here are the best things to do in La Paz.

Snorkel with Whale Sharks and Sea Lions

By far, swimming with the whale shark and sea lions is the biggest must-do activity when visiting La Paz. It is a unique experience worth trying at least once, if not several times during your stay. The friendly giants stay in the bay from January through April.

Tour operators around the city, particularly along the Malecon, are willing to take you to experience magical moments interacting with the biggest shark in the sea. They also provide you the snorkeling equipment and wet suits and some provide full or half-day combination tours.

You can also extend your journey to Isla Espiritu Santo to witness Baja's largest colony of sea lions. The island is a UNESCO biosphere reserve, so there is no restaurant or store, and wildlife thrives in its natural habitat. You must visit the island as part of a tour.

The Mexican government is quite protective of its marine environment. So whether you are swimming with whale sharks or sea lions or exploring La Isla Espiritu Santo, the government requires that you have a proper pass as part of its way to protect the marine life and biosphere of La Paz. These are included in any tours you take.

Wander the Malecon

La Paz has beautiful sunsets, and anywhere along the Malecon is the perfect spot to watch the sun sinking into the sea. Of all of the Malecons in Baja, this is the longest and full of the most activities.

It is quite a popular spot among both locals and tourists. In the morning and evenings, you will see people jogging, walking, exercising and cycling. There are special sections of the Malecon for kids (and adults) to exercise and play or to enjoy a concert or street performer.

Of course, you could eat (or drink) your way from one end of the Malecon to the other. It would take a long time to do so as the Malecon stretches over 2 miles and offers all sorts of food and drink opportunities. Whether you are looking for fine dining, casual eats or street food - it's all along the Malecon.

Plus, the Malecon comes alive during special times. During the Christmas season, for instance, the Malecon will be decorated in lights and Christmas displays and there will be nightly performances attracting crowds of all kinds. And perhaps the most popular time of year for La Paz, during Carnaval, the Malecon is shut down to vehicles and turns into a huge party with nightly parades, games and rides and all sorts of food stalls and art vendors.

Go Diving in the Sea of Cortez
La Paz is an excellent place for scuba diving. It has a rich wildlife and stunning underwater scenery both within the bay and throughout the nearby Sea of Cortez. Scuba diving also allows you to get closer to the whales, whale sharks, sea lions and colorful ocean life of Isla Espiritu Santo.

Tours are readily available in the city. Tour guides provide all the equipment, take you to the dive site and guide you through the dive.

Head Out On A Hike
La Paz has many travel and adventure opportunities, and hiking is one of the top ways to see a side of the region many fail to experience. Some popular hikes in the area include

Balandra Beach

The beach is known for its pristine white sand and crystalline water. It has scenic surroundings with a series of trails that allows you to have a bird's eye view of the beach. You'll begin the hike just south of the Balandra Beach entrance and trek up the hill to where a cell tower stands overlooking the bay. The only better view of Balandra beach is with a drone!

Cerro de la Calavera

A moderate 4-mile out-and-back trail will take you from the northern end of the Malecon to the nearby mountaintop. Here you will explore several caves and arches and experience the most spectacular views overlooking the city and the sunset.

Puerto Mexia

If you have a 4WD or an ATV you can reach the trailhead to this hike that will take you between the desert landscapes and remote seaside beaches. Search the tide pools for all sorts of marine life and enjoy the desert flora and fauna in near isolation.

Other nearby hikes will take a little more effort to reach:

Sierra de la Laguna Mountains

This is a moderate 7-mile out-and-back hike near La Paz. The area is filled with hot springs, hidden lakes, palm trees, waterfalls and river canyons. Moreover, the place is also a habitat for some species of hummingbirds.

Espiritu Santo Island

The island is 18 miles away from the city. It is a part of the UNESCO biosphere reserve and home to an enormous colony of sea lions. With the specialized guide, you can hike around the island to closely observe the wildlife in their natural habitat.

Enjoy Watersports

The calm and shallow water of the beaches near La Paz allows for many watersport activities. Snorkeling, diving, kayaking, fishing, paddleboarding and boating are popular watersport activities you can do at virtually any of the beaches in the area.

In some places, you can literally wade out into the sea from your camping spot with snorkel gear and find yourself exploring a colorful reef within minutes. Of course, as always, respect the marine environment and understand that locals, many of whom will step it up with jet skis and power boats, may not have the same appreciation for the marine environment as you.

Visit World-Famous Beaches

La Paz is home to some of the most incredible beaches in the world. The beaches closer to the town are not the best or most attractive, as La Paz is a commercial port.

If you really want to witness the real Baja beach beauty, Playa Balandra and Playa Tecolote are both within around 30-45 minutes from the city center. They are ideal for swimming, relaxing and enjoying virtually any watersport activities like kayaking and paddle boarding.

At several of these beaches, you can also hire a boat for whale watching and/or a trip to Isla Espiritu Santo. Tour operators will pick you up and drop you off from the beach - which can either be convenient or disruptive to your peace!

Go Sandboarding the dunes of El Mogote Desert

The best and most unique activity in La Paz for adrenaline junkies is sandboarding in the desert. The massive sand dunes of El Mogote offer a different experience of boarding on the sand.

While Baja is a massive desert, the dunes of El Mogote attract the most people to enjoy the unique landscape either by sandboarding or by ATV. You can take your own gear and get out on your own or book any number of tours in town where gear and transportation will be provided.

Hunt for Exceptional Street Art

The streets of La Paz are filled with stunning street art. They are considered cultural landmarks and are featured on what seems like every major street in the city. The local artists make the street art to preserve the city's culture and deep connection with the sea.

Most paintings are of a colorful underwater world gracing the grey walls of streets and buildings. You can walk around the city to experience the fantastic art or book a guided tour to learn more about the meaning and history of different paintings.

Volunteer in La Paz

Kids Up Therapeutic Riding

Within the city limits, Susu has built a wonderful place for equine-assisted therapy classes for local kids with disabilities. Like Horses in Baja in San Felipe, Kids Up uses the soothing nature of horses to help develop kids mentally, emotionally and physically.

You may be able to take part in volunteering in a number of ways. Contact Susu, the owner and operator of Casabuena Bed and Breakfast.

Email: miltuna@gmail.com
Phone: +52 612 122 5538

Nueva Creation Orphanage

The "New Creations" orphanage is located just outside of La Paz and is home to dozens of local area kids who take haven there. Most of the kids live on property during the weekdays and then return to their homes on weekends and holidays. But there is plenty to do around the orphanage, both in sharing your time and activities with the kids and in helping to keep it funded and maintained. Currently the best contact information is through the Squamish BC Rotary Club's website.

Campgrounds in La Paz

Despite its size, strategic location and popularity of the capital city, there is only one formal campground within the city limits. Although it is not near the city center and a bit expensive by Baja standards, this is one of the best campgrounds in the entire peninsula and offers every amenity you will need when camping near La Paz.

Campestre La Maranatha

Address:	Carretera Transpeninsular Km 11 Chametla, 23205 La Paz, B.C.S., Mexico
Website:	https://maranathaministriesinmexico.org/camp-maranatha/
Phone Number:	+52 612 219 6089
GPS Coordinates:	24.098, -110.3871
Price Range:	$25 - 30 USD

Campestre La Maranatha is a large campground that serves as virtually every camper's base camp at some point during your time in La Paz. Whether you make it home and take excursions from the campground or just swing by to do laundry, shower and dump/fill up your tanks - you're going to spend some time at La Maranatha.

The campground has all the amenities you could want or need. With excellent Wi-Fi, hot showers and clean bathrooms, you'll feel as though you are back in the states.

You can also hire services a la carte. Pay for a shower, dump or water refill separate from either dry camping or camping with full hookups.

The staff is incredibly friendly and the campground has a small café. Campestre La Maranatha also has a volleyball and basketball court, a nice pool, a playground for kids, laundry facilities and nice gardens to sit in and enjoy.

Best Boondocking /Alternative Camping Options

Playa el Tecolote

Just a 30-minute drive outside of La Paz, Playa el Tecolote is by far the most popular beach near La Paz to visit and/or camp. Although there is no cellular service at the beach, there is plenty of room to camp along the water's edge or up into the desert if it is crowded.

Camping is free and there will be plenty of vendors selling all sorts of items throughout the day, in addition to a handful of restaurants located at the start of the beach. With views of Isla Espirito Santo just offshore, this beach is a stunning reminder of why you came to Baja in the first place!

Dunas de Mogote

These sand dunes, located just north of La Paz on your way into the city, are world-famous for hosting sandboarding opportunities. As the name suggests, the road in is full of sand and you may be limited in how far down you plan to go.

Although not as popular with the locals, you will likely have a few people come to enjoy sandboarding during your stay. You can also camp at the nearby Playa El Mogote if you don't have the nerve to go further.

Destinations Along the Southern Tip

The southern tip of the Baja Peninsula includes what is considered the "East Cape" stretching from Los Barriles to Los Cabos and the western edge of the peninsula that sides with the Pacific Ocean.

Like the rest of Baja, this area is diverse both in its landscapes as well as activities. From flatwater sports such as kayaking, paddleboarding and fishing to catching waves surfing or riding the wind with a kiteboard, there is no shortage of things to do in this region.

Plus you'll find ample culture and history, delicious food and drink and yes, even a little nightlife if that is what you are seeking. And don't forget the many whale interactions that take place as a handful of different species migrate seasonally around the southern cape between the Pacific Ocean and Sea of Cortez.

La Ventana/El Sargento

La Ventana, or "the window," is a classic Baja California Sur town that has grown a reputation for attracting a certain thrill-seeking kind of traveler. Although the town itself is a traditional fishing village on the coast of the Sea of Cortez, strong winter winds bring windsport fanatics in droves.

This is one of the most popular places in the world for kiteboarding and windsurfing and visiting at the wrong time will likely leave a bad taste in your mouth as the entire area ends up feeling like a beach scene from Point Break.

La Ventana Bay was first developed in 1940 when pearl diver Salome Leon brought his family over the mountains from La Paz because pearl diving became unprofitable. Today, many of his family members and descendants live in the village.

RVING BAJA

There is another small town on the northern end of the bay called El Sargento, which is sort of an extension of La Ventana. Between these two towns, you'll find all you could want - from camping and logistics to adventure and watersports.

La Ventana has a tiny population that almost doubles or even triples between the cold months of November and March. During this period, northerly winds blow in the afternoon creating the perfect environment for kitesurfing.

The La Ventana sky gets filled with colorful kites during this period. Moreover, in season you will find tons of excellent watersport activities when the wind dies down and you can kayak, paddleboard and swim or snorkel the nearby reefs.

From hiking, mountain biking and just relaxing on the beach, La Ventana has many activities for those travelers not interested in kitesurfing. Moreover, you can book a boat ride to the nearby Isla Cerralvo for some fishing, snorkeling and swimming in the Sea of Cortez.

The natural hot springs of Playa Agua Caliente, on the northern end of El Sargento, are also a place not to miss, especially if you are visiting the town in winter. Here you can actually dig your own hot spring in the mud and sand and sit and enjoy the warmth throughout the day.

Things to Do in La Ventana

La Ventana is an adventure outdoor sport and wind sports capital of Baja. Beautiful beaches, crystal clear water, miles of trails in the desert and kiteboarders flying across the bay are the trademark of La Ventana.

Here are the things to do in La Ventana and El Sargento.

Go Kiteboarding

Kiteboarding is the most popular tourist attraction in La Ventana. The northern winds and calm water create an ideal environment in winter. Kite surfers visit in huge numbers to fill the sky with colorful kites and take up most of the camping during the winter months.

But people travel from all over the world to kite surf in La Ventana and it is an excellent spot for both professional and beginner surfers.

All the equipment is readily available at operators throughout the town. Moreover, multiple kitesurfing schools on the bay offer gear rentals and learning opportunities. Some schools also have accommodations and offer multiday packages with lessons.

Build Your Own Hot Springs

Playa Agua Caliente is a natural hot spring located on the northern end of El Sargento. The beach is a perfect spot to take a break and relax in the hot springs that soak from the ground up.

The best time to visit the hot springs is when the tides are low, as they lie right under the sand and pebbles along the shoreline. Here, you'll rearrange some rocks and dig up sand to fill your own personal hot spring. While relaxing, you might also witness some Mobula Rays playing and jumping in the water.

Go Mountain Biking

La Ventana has some of the best mountain biking trails in all of Mexico. There are over 70 trails spanning over 80 miles (130 km) divided into two sections. The south trail passes through the thick Cardon cacti forest on the southern end of La Ventana. The track is comparatively flat and great for beginners.

The north trail goes up to the hills overlooking the Playa Agua Caliente. The local mountain bike association spends lots of time and effort maintaining all the routes.

Moreover, multiple shops in the area offer bike rentals and repairs if needed.

Hike the Punta Gorda Trail
Punta Gorda is a beautiful trail to a scenic rocky beach. It is a 3.6-mile hike showcasing the typical Baja terrain of rocky mountains on one side and shimmering sea on the other. It starts from the hot springs beach and ends at a beautiful and hidden calm rocky beach that is an excellent place for snorkeling.

We recommend starting just before sunrise to enjoy the fantastic views of the sun rising from the Sea of Cortez. Don't forget to pack extra water and snacks because unlike the beaches of La Paz or Bahia Concepcion, there are no shops or restaurants on the beach.

Enjoy Snorkeling
Snorkeling, kayaking, and paddleboarding are popular morning activities just before the wind picks up later in the day. If you haven't brought your own, you can rent gear at local shops.

The reef near an undeveloped beach just north of El Sargento, Bahia de Los Muertos, and Punta Arena are great spots for snorkeling.

Take a Ride to Isla Cerralvo
Isla Cerralvo is an 18-mile-long island just off the coast of La Ventana. It is similar to Espiritu Santo in La Paz but with far fewer tourists visiting it each year. Hiking and snorkeling tours of the island are locally available via boat.

Keep in mind visiting Isla Cerralvo can get complicated in winter because of strong winds.

Campgrounds in La Ventana and El Sargento

There are only a couple of campground options in La Ventana and El Sargento.

El Sargento Beach Campground

Address:	Corredor Isla Cerralvo, 3246+3C
	La Ventana, B.C.S., Mexico
GPS Coordinates:	24.0556, -109.9889
Price Range:	$12 - 15 USD

El Sargento is a basic, but nice beachfront campground that basically offers dry camping. There are very few amenities, but the bathroom and showers are pretty clean. The beach is quite nice, and the water is excellent for snorkeling.

You can also fish on the beach. However, from November to March do not expect to find a decent spot due to the number of kiteboarders in town for the long haul.

Brisa del Mar RV Park

Address:	Calle s/n, 23232 El Sgto, B.C.S., Mexico
Website:	https://www.facebook.com/brisadelmarrvpark/
Phone Number:	+52 612 233 5731
GPS Coordinates:	24.0817, -110.0007
Price Range:	$25 USD

Located away from town, Brisa del Mar RV Park is a rather new campground with full hookups, a hot shower, clean toilets and fast Wi-Fi. It is on a hilltop, so there is no beach, less wind and a much smaller crowd.

There are around a dozen campsites that can support small to mid-size RVs (up to around 30 feet). The park has a communal kitchen area for cooking and stargazing is great here!

Los Barriles

Los Barriles, or "the barrels," is another kitesurfing capital like La Ventana, with the addition of several more campgrounds, loads of places to eat, drink and replenish the supplies and a substantial expat community that kind of makes you feel like you're back home.

People tend to either love or hate Los Barriles due to the many creature comforts you can find here, including the incessant and often annoying drone of ATVs racing through the streets.

The town is located on Las Palmas Bay, almost midway between La Paz (65 miles south) and Los Cabos (65 miles north). With a laid-back vibe and shimmering bay, Los Barriles incorporates the Baja beach culture with tons of watersport activities, wind sailing, snorkeling, and fishing.

Los Barriles has a small permanent population that explodes in winter when northerly winds create the ideal windsurfing conditions that attract travelers from all over the world. Windsurfers and kiteboarders gather to fill the Los Barriles sky with colorful kites and parachutes.

During the off-season, the town is among the most tranquil and calm places in Baja California Sur, a perfect place to sit, relax and live at a slower pace.

Los Barriles mainly has miles of pebble and sand beaches. But a short journey to the north and south takes you to powdery white sand beaches with clear and warm water. Relaxing on the beach, hooking some fish, swimming in the tranquil water and watching marine life in the Sea of Cortez are popular activities here.

There is also the opportunity to go horseback riding on the beach if that's ever been on your bucket list.

Los Barriles is ideal for wind sports from November through March as the wind blows consistently most afternoons. Moreover, Los Barriles beaches are the ground for Baja's biggest kiteboarding exhibition and competition held each year in January.

But it is important to note that with all of the beach activities, a handful of sea turtles nest on these same beaches during late fall and there are signs and markers to indicate when and where it is acceptable to drive on the beach.

Things to Do in Los Barriles

Given the proximity to the desert and Sea of Cortez, the quaint fishing town offers all sorts of activities, from resting and enjoying an escape from the cold northern winters to being as active as you want in outdoor activities.

Here are the things to do in Los Barriles.

Go Fishing

Sportfishing is one of the popular activities in Los Barriles. The Sea of Cortez has an abundance of game fish species and the waters are full of large private fishing boats moored until the waters teem with big game fish. Some popular fish in Los Barriles are snapper, mahi-mahi, roosterfish, yellow tuna and swordfish.

If you don't have your own boat, you can hire a fishing trip in town. Most deep-sea fishing tours are between four to eight hours. And you can also charter big vessels for a full-day tour.

The tour operator provides all the equipment, bait and food. After the tour, you can take your catch to several nearby restaurants to have your fish cooked fresh for you.

Enjoy The Wind Sports

Wind sports season starts in November and lasts through March. During this period, the fast northern breeze becomes ideal for kite-surfing, windsurfing and a variety of spinoff activities that harness the consistently strong wind. It usually blows from mid-morning until late afternoon providing significant hours to practice your skills.

During these months, the town of Los Barriles booms with tourists enjoying the unique weather phenomenon. Many professionals come with their own gear, and kiteboarding schools are open to teaching beginners. Some schools provide accommodation and also teach yoga, kayaking and paddle boarding.

Relax at the Beaches

Playa Los Barriles is a beautiful beach with miles of shoreline. The stunning beach has clear water with various volleyball courts, beach bars and pop-up kite surfing schools. The beach is a mixture of small pebbles and soft sand, so it is not necessarily the most spectacular beach in Baja. But it is well worth enjoying if you are looking to relax.

You can also explore the remote beaches on the north and south of Playa Los Barriles. The beaches have nice powdery white sand with warm and crystal-clear water. These beaches are also typically calm and peaceful.

Accessing the northern and southern beaches is slightly tricky be-cause of the hilly terrain, so renting a 4x4 ATV or a mountain bike is better. There are several ATV rental companies in town as this is one of the more popular activities to do in Los Barriles.

Get Off Road with an ATV or Mountain Bike

Although the main roads in town are paved, the roads just outside of Los Barriles are in pretty bad condition. And many remote beach-es, a hidden waterfall and some other attractions are on nearby hilly terrain. That's why ATVs and mountain bikes are the best mode of transport in and around town.

The rentals are available throughout the town at a handful of shops. You can also hire a guide to take you on informative tours to waterfalls, mango plantations and more remote beaches.

Hike to Cascada Sol del Mayo

Cascada Sol del Mayo is a waterfall located just south of Los Barriles near the village of Santiago, just half an hour to the south. The beautiful place is like an oasis with fresh and clean water pools.

The hike is quite short, less than 1 mile along a steep trail that leads to a 60-foot waterfall. Don't forget to pack your swimsuit if you want to bathe under the waterfall. But note that pets aren't allowed on the trail and there is sometimes a fee to hike the trail.

Volunteer in Los Barriles

Cortez Rescue

Taking advantage of the fact that there are loads of American and Canadian travelers in the area, Cortez Rescue is the leading dog shelter in the East Cape. Located just a few minutes outside of town, the rescue is typically full of dogs awaiting their forever home.

There are lots of ways to volunteer - from simply playing with and walking the dogs to fostering or assisting in airport runs or even being a flight escort for dogs who have been adopted in Canada or the US.

Contact them through their website contact form or connect with them on Facebook.

Campgrounds in Los Barriles

Because Los Barriles attracts so many seasonal visitors, there are several great campground options that range from more high-end resorts to basic dry camping. But the volume of campers also means that you can expect to pay at least $25 USD or more for a full hookup campsite.

Martin Verdugo's Beach Resort

Address:	Apartado Postal 17, 23501 Los Barriles, B.C.S., Mexico
Website:	http://www.verdugosbeachresort.com/
Phone Number:	+52 624 141 0054
GPS Coordinates:	23.6822, -109.6975
Price Range:	$25 - 30 USD

Verdugo's Beach Resort is a huge RV park with a beachfront restaurant and a pool. It is not a big rig-friendly campground (30-32 foot maximum). But it does have clean toilets and showers, fast WiFi and good food at the restaurant.

You'll be packed in pretty tight with other campers, most of whom are likely to be long-term campers during the peak season. There is a narrow gate to enter the campground, so be mindful of your rig as you enter Verdugo's.

East Cape RV Resort

Address:	23330, C. 20 Noviembre 186, 23330 Los Barriles, B.C.S., Mexico
Website:	https://www.bajasresortateastcape.com/
Phone Number:	+52 208 788 2053
GPS Coordinates:	23.6874, -109.6993
Price Range:	$35 USD

Although it is not beachside, East Cape RV Park is an excellent campground located within walking distance of the center of town. The ground is covered with many trees and plants to help provide protection from the wind.

There are fantastic amenities including full hookups, clean bathrooms and even a hot tub. East Cape RV Resort is big-rig friendly.

However, the RV spots are limited to only 18 spaced out between permanent campers and rental bungalows. And while you're not on the water, the popular windsurfing beach is only a 5-minute walk from the campground.

Playa Norte RV Park

Address:	Los Barriles S N, 23330 Los Barriles, B.C.S., Mexico
Phone Number:	+1 (425)252-5952
Website:	https://playanortervpark.com/
GPS Coordinates:	23.7017, -109.7011
Price Range:	$16 - 40 USD

Playa Norte RV Park is another beachfront campground on the northern end of town just past the arroyo and within walking distance from the center of town. The campground is slightly expensive, but the sites are clean, well-maintained and suitable for big rigs.

Moreover, the toilets are clean and the staff is friendly. One great thing about Playa Norte is that there is reasonably priced dry camping available ($16 USD) and they offer a dump station to use for a few dollars.

Best Boondocking /Alternative Camping Option

Arroyo San Bartolo

The arroyo, or dry river bed, just to the north of town is by far the most popular place to boondock in Los Barriles. There are hundreds of places that will tend to fill up quickly in the fall and winter months as kiteboarders flock to free living on the East Cape.

Follow any number of tracks through the sand toward the sea and set up camp as close to the water as you can get. We do advise you to walk the track before if you do not have a vehicle with 4WD as there will be patches of soft sand along the way. From here it is a short 20-30 minute walk into town either along the beach or roads.

Cabo Pulmo

Cabo Pulmo is a dusty little town located on the southeast corner of Baja California Sur, a truly hidden gem as the road in and out rules out most larger RVs. Although we recommend that everyone put Cabo Pulmo on their Baja bucket list, getting in and out of the area is a real challenge - particularly with larger vehicles and RVs.

The small village of Cabo Pulmo, with less than 200 residents, has done a lot to preserve the wildlife of the Sea of Cortez as it is within the Cabo Pulmo National Park.

The town feels a world away from the glitz and glam of Cabo San Lucas and San Jose del Cabo. And even compared to Los Barriles, Cabo Pulmo is but a small village preserved in time.

As Jacques Cousteau once described the Sea of Cortez as the "Aquarium of the World," due to the abundance of species found in it. And Cabo Pulmo National Park has taken the lead in recent years to preserve the beauty and diversity of marine life, shifting the economic focus from fishing to ecotourism.

Despite being very close to some major cities like La Paz and Cabo San Lucas, the National Reserve is very unspoiled. There are a handful of small restaurants, no ATMs or Wi-Fi, and all roads in and out of the village are unpaved and hardly ever maintained.

The laid-back vibe and stunning natural beauty of the remote region of Cabo Pulmo really attract people looking to see Baja the way it might have been 30 or 40 years ago.

Cabo Pulmo is the home to the only living hard coral reef in the Sea of Cortez. It is estimated to be around 20,000 years old and lies over 50 feet below the water's surface. The reef provides the perfect environment for a huge variety of tropical fish, sea mammals, seabirds and marine plants.

The Mexican government declared the 70 square km area around Cabo Pulmo to be a federally protected national reserve and UNESCO declared it a world heritage site in 2005.

The nutrient-rich warm waters of the national reserve are a perfect place for scuba diving and snorkeling. Multiple diving spots are wonderful and have the most diverse marine environment in all of Baja.

In addition to marine beauty, the land of Cabo Pulmo is equally beautiful. It has some of the most stunning remote beaches and numerous hikes that allow you to enjoy the bird's eye view of Cabo Pulmo and the Marine Reserve.

Things to Do in Cabo Pulmo

The best activities in Cabo Pulmo involve actually getting into the Sea of Cortez. But there is plenty to discover in the small town as well.

Here are the things to do in Cabo Pulmo.

Go Snorkeling and Scuba Diving

Cabo Pulmo is one of the best diving sites in the world. The pristine reef, clear water, and vast wildlife attract divers from all over the world. You can dive year-round. But the best time to enjoy this part of the Sea of Cortez is between September and November as the water is warm and the visibility is at its best.

Several dive shops offer dives for certified divers. Possible sighting includes bull sharks, reef sharks, jackfish, sea turtles, occasional whales and all varieties of tropical fish.

You are also welcome to snorkel virtually anywhere you find suitable. Our favorite activity in Cabo Pulmo is to load up our snorkeling gear on our paddleboards and head out to find a more remote reef away from the crowds. Just be mindful not to disturb the coral or marine life if you go unguided.

Enjoy a Hike

The ocean isn't the only attraction. There are a few marked trails around the town and numerous others you can find on your own near any of the beaches. Perhaps the most popular hike is to the tower on the top of the hill that overlooks the small village and surrounding areas.

A very rough road takes you to the mountain and a 30-minute hike will provide you with an aerial view of the national park and lush landscape of Cabo Pulmo.

Get a Paddle In - Kayaking and Paddle Boarding

Kayaking and paddle boarding are great activities that you can do without a guide in Cabo Pulmo. If you don't own your own, both kayaks and paddleboards are readily available at local shops.

Start in the morning and look for mother humpback whales with their calves, Mobula rays jumping out of the water to impress the females and sharks and tropical fish cruising around in the deep waters.

Campgrounds in Cabo Pulmo National Park

There are no formal campgrounds within Cabo Pulmo National Park. However, there are several informal areas to camp and a few private properties that offer overnight parking.

Some of the more popular places include the beaches near the town of Cabo Pulmo and Los Arbolitos and Los Frailes to the south of town.

Do be mindful of soft sand, rocky roads and constant erosion and potholes that can be catastrophic for RVs, trailers and vehicles of all kinds.

Todos Santos

Todos Santos is an artistic and culturally rich town with a laid-back vibe located on the Pacific Ocean. It is almost equal distance (around 50 miles/80 km) from both La Paz and Cabo San Lucas, making it ripe for tourists passing from one city to the other.

There is also a large community of ex-pats developing higher-end residences that sprawl from the town center along the Pacific Ocean. This has created another place where you can find most of the amenities and comforts of home you may need while camping in the area.

However, despite the proximity and influence of the larger cities, Todos Santos has a unique small-town feel to it. Home to the "Hotel California" (not officially related to the Eagle's famous song), Todos Santos is a haven for artists and travelers alike. Many of the streets are paved in cobblestone and the architecture of the buildings reflects its colonial past.

Like many other population centers in Baja, Todos Santos was founded in 1723 by Jesuit missionaries in the area. The missionary took advantage of the fertile land and started planting sugarcane. In the 19th century, the small town had eight sugar mills.

But in the 1950s, the spring dried up and all the mills were closed by 1965. After devastating years, the spring came back to life in 1981.

In the 1980s, the Mexican government paved Highway 19 to bring tourists to the area. Both developments played a vital role in the economy of Todos Santos.

The locals moved from farming sugarcane and planted vegetables, chilies, avocados, papayas, and mangos. Further, the paved highway shifted the financial dependency on tourism and real estate. Fishing, ranching, and local art also significantly share the local economy.

Todos Santos is also known as an artist's colony because of the abundance of art galleries in the town. The locals are quite artistic and also sell their art at affordable prices primarily to tourists that come from Cabo San Lucas.

Most of the town is inland. But the outskirts of Todos Santos touch the Pacific coast where you can enjoy signature Baja activities like kayaking, surfing, fishing and snorkeling. The town also has some hiking trails in the nearby Sierra Laguna Mountains.

Things to Do in Todos Santos

Todos Santos is a unique desert oasis surrounded by lush green orchards overlooking the spectacular views of white sand beaches and the Pacific Ocean.

Here are the things to do in Todos Santos.

Go Surfing

Although you have to go a little outside of town to reach the ocean, surfing in Todos Santos ends up on nearly every surfer's bucket list. The most popular palace to surf is La Pastora, a wide-open dirt field about 10 minutes north of town along a mostly dirt road.

Also, Playa Los Cerritos and Playa San Pedrito are great places for surfing. They are 20 minutes away from the town and have both gentle and adventurous rocky point breaks, which makes them an excellent place for beginners and professionals alike.

You can rent surfboards and wetsuits around town and some vendors also offer lessons.

Take A Walk Through History

Downtown Todos Santos is an exciting and historical place. Most of its building and cobblestone streets were built in the 19th century during the sugarcane boom. The colorful facade of colonial buildings still fill with local residents and businesses alike.

Moreover, Mision Nuestra Senora del Pilar de Todos Santos is also downtown. Built in 1733, it was the first mission in the area and has a great view of the nearby area.

Pick any street and wander to your heart's content. Grab a "Taco de Cabeza" (yes, "head taco"), a local specialty sold by most street vendors, or pick any number of restaurants or bars to enjoy a variety of food and drink.

Todos Santos is one of those towns where people-watching is at its finest and you can spend an entire day strolling the cobblestone streets and enjoying the various shops and vendors along the way.

Release Baby Sea Turtles in the Sea

Releasing baby sea turtles safely in the ocean is a magical experience. The beaches around Todos Santos are a nesting ground for three types of sea turtles (Olive Ridleys, Leatherbacks, and Black Sea Turtles).

Hatching season starts in December through April and Tortugueros Las Playitas, a non-profit sea turtle sanctuary manages the endangered species year-round. Every evening volunteers collect recently laid turtle eggs from nests along the nearby beach and move them into a protected hatchery, where the turtles can be incubated and hatch on their own.

You can visit Torugueros Las Playitas every day and releasing newly hatched turtles is free to the public. Be sure to head down before sunset as the turtles are released just after sunset, when they have the best chance of surviving attacks from predators.

You'll likely experience a spectacular sunset over the Pacific Ocean and may even see whales breaching while you await the release.

Go Whale Watching

Todos Santos is an excellent place to see grey and humpback whales migrating around the southern tip of Baja during the winter months. Humpback whales travel from October through January and grey whales migrate between January and March.

Whale-watching tours are readily available in the town and nearby beaches. But if you want to save a few bucks, you can watch the whales play from any beach while enjoying sunset or surfing.

Hike to Punta Lobos

Punta Lobos is a popular spot located just 3 miles (5 km) from the center of Todos Santos. A mostly secluded beach, Punta Lobos also has a hiking trail that takes you to spectacular views overlooking the ocean.

The trail to the top is not well marked. And once on top, you will be on the edge of the cliff so be mindful of your steps while you enjoy the views.

Volunteer in Todos Santos

Tortugueros Las Playitas

This sea turtle rescue is among the premiere in Baja, where a variety of sea turtles come ashore by the thousands to lay eggs. The organization is responsible for gathering freshly laid turtle eggs and relocating them to a hatchery where the eggs can incubate and hatch without interference from predators.

Each night, as long as there is a batch of turtles ready to go, newly hatched sea turtles are released into the sea at sunset. You can volunteer either by releasing a turtle and making a donation or you can contact the organization about being the biologist of the day, where you will assist in everything from collecting the eggs to monitoring the hatchery and interacting with visitors throughout the day.

Website: http://www.todostortugueros.org/
Email: tortugueroslasplayitas@gmail.com

Ecorrrevolucion

Ecorrrevolution is a non-governmental agency started by a man named Alex, who wanted to help reduce the environmental impact of those people living in Todos Santos. Alex collects a variety of recyclable materials and sorts them into those items that can be recycled with similar materials and those that are trash.

He is constantly looking for help both with fundraising as well as sorting the daily materials, which locals and gringos alike drop off by the bagfull each day.

Website: https://www.ecorrrevolucion.org/
Phone: +52 1 612 139 4789

Campgrounds in Todos Santos

There are not a lot of options for camping in Todos Santos. In fact, there is only one campground in town and it is quite the opposite of what you would expect in such a fine town.

We had a terrible experience here, as have numerous other people, and we hesitated to even include it in this guide.

However, if you want to camp in Todos Santos proper to be able to enjoy the town without having to drive in from nearby boondocking sites, El Litro RV Park is your only option.

El Litro RV Park

Address:	Francisco Bojorquer Vidal, San Vicente, 23300 Todos Santos, B.C.S., Mexico
Phone Number:	+52 612 200 7580
Website:	http://todossantosguide.com/ellitrorvpark/index.html
GPS Coordinates:	23.4406, -110.227
Price Range:	$12 - 15 USD

El Litro RV Park is located at the edge of Todos Santos, a dirt lot ringed with palm trees. Overall, the place is not well managed. But its location is what attracts most campers.

It does have electrical hookups (though there were lots of exposed wires and we recommend you have a surge protector if plugging in) and a common shower area (that is not well maintained).

But aside from basic amenities, you're paying a premium for the location, not for the quality of the campground.

Best Boondocking /Alternative Camping Option

La Pastora

La Pastora is a wide open field that virtually anyone who travels and boondocks to Baja California Sur knows about. It is particularly popular among surfers as it is home to some of the consistently best surf around Todos Santos.

The road in is a little bumpy and be mindful of when it may rain as the field is mostly dirt, which turns into an awfully slick and soft material in the rain. Also note that if you attempt to go too far toward the ocean you may find yourselves stuck in the soft sand.

However, this is your best opportunity to camp around Todos Santos and there will be plenty of space to park for the night, even if the waves are going off.

El Pescadero / Playa Los Cerritos

El Pescadero is a developing village about 8 miles from Todos Santos and 50 miles (80 km) North of Cabo San Lucas. Combined with its neighboring beach, Playa Los Cerritos, the area has the perfect blend of super friendly people, delicious food and the basics to support a few days of camping in the area.

It has quickly become the neighboring alternative to Todos Santos, where you can be close enough to visit Todos Santos whenever you'd like but be in a lesser developed and more affordable area.

The village of El Pescadero was first inhabited in 1724 by the same missionaries who developed Todos Santos. Although its name translates to "fishmonger" or "fish buyer," El Pescadero is actually located several miles inland from the Pacific Ocean.

The area is famous for chilies and basil leaves. However, juicy mangoes, sweet strawberries, cherry tomatoes and papayas are also a big part of the local farming industry. Farming around Pescadero flourishes because of the underground water funneled down from the Sierra de la Laguna mountains.

El Pescadero and Playa Los Cerritos have remained relatively undeveloped for a significant time. But the increasing popularity among ex-pats from US and Canada has led to rather quick development in the area.

Around Pescadero, especially on the Pacific side of the village where the village combines with Playa Los Cerritos, there is an increasing number of homes, bed and breakfasts and hotels. And more and more businesses and restaurants are opening throughout the area.

Nearby Playa Los Cerritos is the oceanfront community that offers a beautiful beach with excellent surfing and fishing. More and more restaurants and bars are popping up and this beach has become the go-to for visitors to Todos Santos who are looking to rent a palapa or surfboard to spend the day relaxing in the sun.

Although unaffiliated, this region has become the "suburbs" of Todos Santos and offers far more opportunities to camp than in Todos Santos.

Things to Do in El Pescadero and Los Cerritos

Although Pescadero and Los Cerritos lack the charm of other villages and towns in Baja, there are still plenty of reasons to visit.

Here are the things to do in Pescadero.

Head Out Surfing

Playa Cerritos is among the most popular places to surf in Baja California Sur. The coast has both gentle and rocky breakpoints, making it an excellent spot for professionals and beginners.

Surfing equipment is readily available on the beach and there are a few surf schools on-site that offer lessons. Most people surf along the point beneath the big hotel at the north end of the beach because it creates waves that span out to the right and go a long way down the beach.

Enjoy Sportfishing

Sportfishing is another popular attraction in Pescadero. You will likely head out from Punta Lobos, a small beach just north of Pescadero. Local fishermen will take you to the best places to catch fish on half or full-day excursions.

If you are craving fresh seafood and don't want to catch it yourself, you can often buy fish at Punta Lobos and take it back to cook where you are camping.

Relax at the Beach

Playa Los Cerritos is a sandy beach with generally gentle waves. Although there are times when swells will create large waves, Cerritos is a hugely popular place because it is safe to swim most days of the year.

In fact, vendors line the alleyways to the ocean and sell all sorts of items to make your stay more relaxing. From surfboard and wetsuit rentals to all sorts of food, you can arrive in Cerritos with nothing and still make a great day of it.

And if relaxing is your number one priority, there are palapas that you can rent for some shade when you want it and plenty of people will come around and offer massages right there on the beach.

Wear Yourself Out With Water Sports

When the surf is not up, the calm waters of Playa Los Cerritos offer the opportunity to head out on the water kayaking and paddleboarding. So regardless of whether you camp in the area so you can surf or paddle, you can wear yourself out virtually every day of the week doing one water sport or the other.

Plus, during winter, humpback and grey whales migrate close to shore and you may have some encounters if you time your paddle. While it's rare to come very close to whales offshore, do be mindful of the sheer size of the whales and enjoy watching them from a distance.

Campgrounds in Pescadero

As the growing alternative to Todos Santos, El Pescadero offers more camping opportunities than anywhere else around. In fact, it seems as if every year there is at least one new campground opening up to support the increasing number of visitors to the area.

Most campgrounds are closer to Pescadero, inland from Cerritos, due to the affordability of the land. But these campgrounds, as with other developments in the area, tend to cascade up the desert hills away from the ocean providing spectacular views of the ocean even though they are not oceanfront.

Casa Caravan

Address:	Carretera, Degollado Km 65, Playa Cerritos, 23310 El Pescadero, B.C.S., Mexico
Website:	https://www.casacaravanbaja.com/
Phone Number:	+1 (678) 447-8024
GPS Coordinates:	23.3432, -110.1686
Price Range:	$30 USD

Casa Caravan is a handy campground just a mile away from Playa Cerritos. Although it is a small campground, it has full hookups, the nicest bathrooms of any campground in Baja, an outdoor kitchen a small pool and a common area that fills up with social campers most nights of the week.

Although many of the spots are a tight fit, the campground is big-rig friendly. However, expect very little privacy as most sites sort of overlap with each other. If you are traveling during winter be sure to reserve a site well in advance as there are many long-term campers who occupy most of the sites through the busy season.

Pescadero Surf Camp

Address:	Carretera, Degollado km 64 El Pescadero, B.C.S., Mexico
Website:	http://pescaderosurf.com/
Phone Number:	+52 612 134 0480
GPS Coordinates:	23.3554, -110.1648
Price Range:	$15 USD

Pescadero Surf Camp is the original campground in Pescadero. It is a beautifully manicured campground with a lovely swimming pool. Although it is not close to the beach, the campground offers amenities that attract all sorts of campers. From fast Wi-Fi, hot showers, clean bathrooms, a public kitchen and the ability to hook up while camping.

However, Pescadero Surf Camp is designed more for smaller RVs and vans and those travelers who want to pitch a tent or rent a room rather than for larger RVs and travel trailers. If you have a Class C RV or larger you'll want to take a pass on camping here.

Cerritos Boutique RV Park

Address:	lote 2191 z1 p1 18, Cerritos Ave s n, 23300 El Pescadero, B.C.S., Mexico
Website:	www.cerritosbrv.com/
GPS Coordinates:	23.3309, -110.1708
Price Range:	$30 USD

Cerritos Boutique RV Park is another relatively expensive but fully equipped campground option close to Cerritos beach. The owner is amiable and overall amenities are great.

Despite being a costly campground, it does not have a pool, unlike the other two campgrounds.

However, you can expect full hookups at every site, spacious and clean bathrooms with hot water, fast WiFi and a communal kitchen.

Cabo San Lucas

Cabo San Lucas is a resort city located on the southern tip of Baja, California. It is the place where the Sea of Cortez and the Pacific Ocean meet, offering all sorts of spectacular beauty that has been enjoyed for decades.

But do know up front that the city is NOT RV-friendly and there are no campgrounds within a reasonable distance of Cabo San Lucas to make staying in the city an option.

The city was once a sleepy fishing village, but the abundance of game fish made it one of the top tourist destinations in Mexico. It is known for its incredible sportfishing, scuba diving, buzzing nightlife, beautiful beaches, delicious food and abundant marine life.

Cabo San Lucas became the most successful beach resort in Baja. A once sleepy fish village now has 5-star resorts along the pristine beaches, world-class restaurants, wild nightclubs, golf courses, unrivaled fishing facilities, cruise ships and lots of international flights each day.

In short, the resort city has everything for everyone. It has adventure sports for adrenaline junkies, incredible food for foodies, romantic beaches for couples, and tons of game fish for fishing enthusiasts. Making it an excellent spot for couples, groups of friends, and families.

Moreover, the moderate weather attracts visitors at all times of the year. The average temperature is 78 degrees, which gets a little cooler or warmer depending on the season.

Golfers from around the world have also added a layer of recreation to Cabo San Lucas. It has ten world-class golf courses designed by the best in the business, including Jack Nicklaus, Robert Trent, Tom Weiskopf and Greg Norman.

Quality and affordable meals are trademarks of Cabo San Lucas and the city has quietly become a place for food lovers. Almost every cuisine in the world is sold on street food stands, beachfront and posh cliffside restaurants. Moreover, fresh seafood is the signature item of Cabo San Lucas.

In addition to city activities, the beaches are also one of a kind. Playa Medano is an excellent spot to sunbathe. As is Playa del Amor (the Lover's beach), a romantic and peaceful place for couples. Moreover, the city is surrounded by stunning and quiet coves on both Pacific and Sea of Cortez shorelines.

Water activities in Cabo San Lucas are truly endless. From scuba diving, kayaking, surfing, jet skiing, boating, whale watching, boat cruises and parasailing - if you can name it, the city has the facilities.

Quad buggies, ATVs, and mountain bike rides in the nearby desert are excellent activities to spend a non-soggy day in Cabo San Lucas. You can also race in go-karts or rent bicycles to explore the city's streets.

Sportfishing is unparalleled in the waters around Cabo San Lucas. It is considered one of the best all-around fishing locations in the world due to the mixture of the Sea of Cortez and the Pacific Ocean keeping the water warm throughout the year.

From landing your first marlin to catching any number of bottom fish, Cabo San Lucas is nothing less than a treasure for fishing lovers.

Things to Do in Cabo San Lucas

Filled with natural landmarks, the city of Cabo San Lucas has a lot of character, particularly on its coastline. It has plenty of entertainment for couples and families alike.

So if you're looking to make a day trip out of Cabo San Lucas, or feel like renting an Airbnb or hotel for a few nights to give camping a break, there is plenty to keep you entertained.

Here are things to do in Cabo San Lucas.

Go Fishing

Cabo San Lucas is very well known for its incredible sport fishing. The city is in a perfect location where diverse ocean life thrives throughout the year. The bay has Blue, Black, and striped Marlins, sailfish, dorado, tuna, wahoo, roosterfish and an endless variety of bottom fish.

Fishing tours are available throughout the city. If hiring a private charter is too expensive, you can choose a fisherman from the local panga fleet. Surf fishing is also quite productive here.

Visit Land's End Arch

Land's End Arch is a beautiful rock formation on an island located at the southernmost end of Cabo San Lucas. It is arguably the most identifiable landmark in Cabo San Lucas, if not all of Baja, and is a peaceful spot to see the sunset with sea lions.

The island is only accessible by a water taxi from the downtown marina. It is the point where the Sea of Cortez and the Pacific Ocean meet, so currents are strong, and swimming is not encouraged in the area.

Head Out Whale Watching

Like many other Baja cities, whale watching is also a popular attraction in Cabo San Lucas. The visiting time of grey and humpback whales is between December and April.

Boats are readily available in the city and along the marina offering tours varying from 2 hours to an entire day.

Enjoy Watersports

Cabo San Lucas has some of the best watersports facilities in the entire Baja. Medano beach is the busiest beach, which makes it an excellent place for parasailing, windsurfing, kayaking, paddle boarding and jet skiing.

Snorkeling on hidden beaches and coves like Playa del Amor is favorable because of the smaller crowds.

Similarly, Cabo Pulmo marine reserve just to the north is a great area to dive or snorkel with marine life.

And Zipper Beach is another excellent location for surfing. The rocky outcrops maintain ideal conditions for surfing throughout the year — though this should be for intermediate and expert surfers. Locals also conduct a surfing competition every summer.

Catch a Sunrise or Sunset at Mount Solmar

Mount Solmar is the best spot to see the sunrise and sunset in Cabo San Lucas. The hill is the highest spot in the city and provides exceptional views of downtown Cabo San Lucas and beaches.

The trail is relatively easy to complete, but remember your sunscreen and pack some water and snacks to keep yourself fueled for the hike.

Campgrounds in Cabo San Lucas

At the time of writing, there are no formal campgrounds in Cabo San Lucas. This makes visiting the city a challenge unless you plan to camp in nearby areas and have a separate vehicle you can use to make trips into the city.

However, there are quite a few informal camping spots as you head toward Cabo Pulmo at the beaches near San Jose del Cabo. Similarly, camping in El Pescadero and Los Cerritos leaves you close enough to make a short trip down to Cabo San Lucas if you want.

Made in the USA
Las Vegas, NV
31 December 2023

83728746R00142